6/05

The Geography of China

The History and Culture of China

Mason Crest Publishers   Philadelphia

Jia Lu

The Geography of China

The History and Culture of China

Mason Crest Publishers   Philadelphia

Jia Lu

Produced by OTTN Publishing, Stockton, New Jersey

Mason Crest Publishers
370 Reed Road
Broomall, PA 19008
www.masoncrest.com

First printing

1 3 5 7 9 8 6 4 2

Library of Congress Cataloging-in-Publication Data

Lu, Jia.
  The geography of China / Jia Lu.
      p. cm. — (History and culture of China)
  Includes bibliographical references and index.
  ISBN 1-59084-828-4
  1. China—Geography. I. Title. II. Series.
  DS706.7.L58 2005
  915.1—dc22
                          2004019890

Table of Contents

Introduction

Dr. Jianwei Wang
University of Wisconsin–Stevens Point

Before his first official visit to the United States in December 2003, Chinese premier Wen Jiabao granted a lengthy interview to the *Washington Post*. In that interview, he observed: "If I can speak very honestly and in a straightforward manner, I would say the understanding of China by some Americans is not as good as the Chinese people's understanding of the United States." Needless to say, Mr. Wen is making a sweeping generalization here. From my personal experience and observation, some Americans understand China at least as well as some Chinese understand the United States. But overall there is some truth in Mr. Wen's remarks. For example, if you visited a typical high school in China, you would probably find that students there know more about the United States than their American counterparts know about China. For one thing, most Chinese teenagers start learning English in high school, while only a very small fraction of American high school students will learn Chinese.

In a sense, the knowledge gap between Americans and Chinese about each other is understandable. For the

Chinese, the United States is the most important foreign country, representing not just the most developed economy, unrivaled military might, and the most advanced science and technology, but also a very attractive political and value system, which many Chinese admire. But for Americans, China is merely one of many foreign countries. As citizens of the world's sole superpower, Americans naturally feel less compelled to learn from others. The Communist nature of the Chinese polity also gives many Americans pause. This gap of interest in and motivation to learn about the other side could be easily detected by the mere fact that every year tens of thousands of Chinese young men and women apply for a visa to study in the United States. Many of them decide to stay in this country. In comparison, many fewer Americans want to study in China, let alone live in that remote land.

Nevertheless, for better or worse, China is becoming more and more important to the United States, not just politically and economically, but also culturally. Most notably, the size of the Chinese population in the United States has increased steadily. China-made goods as well as Chinese food have become a part of most Americans' daily life. China is now the third-largest trade partner of the United States and will be a huge market for American goods and services. China is also one of the largest creditors, with about $100 billion in U.S. government securities. Internationally China could either help or hinder American foreign policy in the United Nations, on issues ranging from North Korea to non-proliferation of weapons of mass destruction. In the last century, misperception of this vast country cost the United States dearly in the Korean War and the Vietnam War. On the issue of Taiwan, China and the United States may once again embark on a collision course if both sides are not careful in handling the dispute. Simply put, the state of U.S.-China relations may well shape the future not just for Americans and Chinese, but for the world at large as well.

The main purpose of this series, therefore, is to help high school students form an accurate, comprehensive, and balanced understanding of China, past and present, good and bad, success and failure, potential and limit, and culture and state. At least three major images will emerge from various volumes in this series.

First is the image of traditional China. China has the longest continuous civilization in the world. Thousands of years of history produced a rich and sophisticated cultural heritage that still influences today's China. While this ancient civilization is admired and appreciated by many Chinese as well as foreigners, it can also be heavy baggage that makes progress in China difficult and often very costly. This could partially explain why China, once the most advanced country in the world, fell behind during modern times. Foreign encroachment and domestic trouble often plunged this ancient nation into turmoil and war. National rejuvenation and restoration of the historical greatness is still considered the most important mission for the Chinese people today.

Second is the image of Mao's China. The establishment of the People's Republic of China in 1949 marked a new era in this war-torn land. Initially the Communist regime was quite popular and achieved significant accomplishments by bringing order and stability back to Chinese society. When Mao declared that the "Chinese people stood up" at Tiananmen Square, "the sick man of East Asia" indeed reemerged on the world stage as a united and independent power. Unfortunately, Mao soon plunged the country into endless political campaigns that climaxed in the disastrous Cultural Revolution. China slipped further into political suppression, diplomatic isolation, economic backwardness, and cultural stagnation.

Third is the image of China under reform. Mao's era came to an abrupt end after his death in 1976. Guided by Deng Xiaoping's farsighted and courageous policy of reform and openness, China has experienced earth-shaking changes in the last quarter century. With the adoption of a market economy, China has transformed itself into a global economic powerhouse in only two decades. China has also become a full-fledged member of the international community, as exemplified by its return to the United Nations and its accession to the World Trade Organization. Although China is far from being democratic as measured by Western standards, overall it is now a more humane place to live, and the Chinese people have begun to enjoy unprecedented freedom in a wide range of social domains.

These three images of China, strikingly different, are closely related with one another. A more sophisticated and balanced perception of China needs to take into consideration all three images and the process of their evolution from one to another, thus acknowledging the great progress China has made while being fully aware that it still has a long way to go. In my daily contact with Americans, I quite often find that their views of China are based on the image of traditional China and of China under Mao—they either discount or are unaware of the dramatic changes that have taken place. Hopefully this series will allow its readers to observe the following realities about China.

First, China is not black and white, but rather—like the United States—complex and full of contradictions. For such a vast country, one or two negative stories in the media often do not represent the whole picture. Surely the economic reforms have reduced many old problems, but they have also created many new problems. Not all of these problems, however, necessarily prove the guilt of the Communist system. Rather, they may be the result of the very reforms the government has been implementing and of the painful transition from one system to another. Those who would view China through a single lens will never fully grasp the complexity of that country.

Second, China is not static. Changes are taking place in China every day. Anyone who lived through Mao's period can attest to how big the changes have been. Every time I return to China, I discover something new. Some things have changed for the better, others for the worse. The point I want to make is that today's China is a very dynamic society. But the development in China has its own pace and logic. The momentum of changes comes largely from within rather than from without. Americans can facilitate but not dictate such changes.

Third, China is neither a paradise nor a hell. Economically China is still a developing country with a very low per capita GDP because of its huge population. As the Chinese premier put it, China may take another 100 years to catch up with the United States. China's political system remains authoritarian and can be repressive and arbitrary. Chinese people still do not have as much freedom as American people enjoy, particularly when it comes to expressing opposition to the government. So China is certainly not an ideal society, as its leaders used to believe (or at least declare). Yet the Chinese people as a whole are much better off today than they were 20 years ago, both economically and politically. Chinese authorities were fond of telling the Chinese people that Americans lived in an abyss of misery. Now every Chinese knows that this is nonsense. It is equally ridiculous to think of the Chinese in a similar way.

Finally, China is both different from and similar to the United States. It is true that the two countries differ greatly in terms of political and social systems and cultural tradition. But it is also true that China's program of reform and openness has made these two societies much more similar. China is largely imitating the United States in many aspects. One can easily detect the convergence of the two societies in terms of popular culture, values, and lifestyle by walking on the streets of Chinese cities like Shanghai. With ever-growing economic and other functional interactions, the two countries have also become increasingly interdependent. That said, it is naïve to expect that China will become another United States. Even if China becomes a democracy one day, these two great nations may still not see eye to eye on many issues.

Understanding an ancient civilization and a gigantic country such as China is always a challenge. If this series kindles readers' interest in China and provides them with systematic information and thoughtful perspectives, thus assisting their formation of an informed and realistic image of this fascinating country, I am sure the authors of this series will feel much rewarded.

A rider guides his horse through a green field in China's fertile Gansu Province. China is one of the world's largest countries, and it includes a variety of terrains, climates, and geographic features.

1

Overview

In eastern Asia, situated between the Yellow and East China Seas to the east and Central Asia to the west, and between Russia to the north and the South China Sea to the south, is a giant land whose shape vaguely resembles that of a chicken. This is China, the world's most populous country, which in mid-2004 was estimated to be home to nearly 1.3 billion people.

Geography and Culture

In addition to its huge population, China ranks as one of the world's largest countries by area. With approximately 3.7 million square miles (9.6 million square kilometers) of territory, China makes up about 6.5 percent of earth's total land area. Some sources list it as the world's third-largest country, behind Russia and Canada; others place China fourth, behind the United States as well.

China boasts one of the oldest uninterrupted civilizations, extending back some 4,000 years. Much of the area within the country's present-day borders was first brought into a unified empire in the third century B.C. Since that time, China has experienced periods of chaos and civil wars, but it has always managed to reunite into a single country.

Over the centuries, as China's territory expanded, its culture and politics spread into nearby lands. The Chinese cultural influence can be seen particularly in Japan, Korea, Vietnam, and Mongolia. Yet throughout the more than two millennia between the founding of its first unified dynasty and the collapse of dynastic rule in the early 20th century, Chinese civilization developed in relative isolation. In part this is due to geography: to the west lie extremely rugged mountains and deserts that were not easily traversed; to the east is the vast Pacific Ocean. In part, however, China's cultural isolation was self-imposed. China traditionally considered itself the center of the civilized world, surrounded by barbarians who had little to offer in cultural terms. This idea is reflected in the name the Chinese used to describe their land: Zhongguo, meaning "Central Kingdom" or "Middle Kingdom."

China's historical isolation is perhaps best symbolized by—indeed, to some extent was actually achieved through—its most recognized landmark: the Great Wall. This ancient wonder, extending some 3,730 miles (6,000 km) across northern China, from Jiayuguan in the northwest to Laolongtou ("Old Dragon Head") along the Bo Sea coast in Hebei Province, is the largest man-made structure ever built. Its walls average about 25 feet (7.8 meters) high and 19 feet (5.8 meters) thick—wide enough for ancient Chinese soldiers to march, or even ride in horse-drawn wagons, along the top. At regular intervals were living quarters for garrisoning soldiers, as well as huge fireplaces where signal fires could be lit to transmit news of an enemy invasion and call for reinforcements.

This map shows the location of China within Asia.

Construction of the Great Wall began during the reign of Qin Shihuang (221–210 B.C.), the first emperor to rule a unified China, and continued sporadically through successive dynasties into the Ming period (A.D. 1368–1644). Qin Shihuang actually began the project by linking together existing defensive walls built by the various Chinese states he had conquered; his purpose was to prevent invasions by the nomadic hordes of "barbarians," known as

U.S. president Richard M. Nixon and his wife, Pat, pose on the Great Wall of China during their historic 1972 visit. The Great Wall, whose construction began in the third century B.C., is one of China's most recognizable landmarks.

Xiongnu, who periodically swept down from the grasslands to China's north. While the Great Wall may have been intended to keep the barbarians out, it also in effect kept the Chinese in, thereby reinforcing China's sense of cultural isolation.

Over the centuries, many parts of the Great Wall have deteriorated or been destroyed. But some sections—such as the one near Beijing, which was refurbished around the 14th century during the Ming dynasty—remain in good condition and serve as a magnet for visitors, including foreign dignitaries.

A Land of Varied Climates

China's climate varies dramatically from region to region. The country includes tropical, subtropical, temperate-warm, temperate, continental, and highland climate regions. On Hainan Island and the adjacent Leizhou Peninsula, and in Yunnan Province in south China, high temperatures and humidity year-round mean that residents experience no winter season. Around the Lower Yangtze River Basin and the Lower Yellow River Basin in eastern China, however, residents enjoy four seasons each year. Winter is especially harsh in Heilongjiang Province in China's extreme northeast, where high amounts of snow fall annually. The vast, less populated deep interior of China experiences great extremes of temperature between winter and summer and between day and night. In China's southwest mountain and valley areas, the climate varies depending on altitude.

These great differences in climate mean that while the people of Harbin in northern China are enjoying ice sculptures, the people of Guangzhou (Canton) in southern China may still be watching roses bloom in their gardens. The temperature in Harbin can drop as low as −40°F (−40°C), and it stays below freezing for almost half the year. Rather than complain about the cold, residents of Harbin celebrate it instead. Each year they hold an outdoor festival of snow and ice sculpture competitions.

Temperature contrasts between seasons of the year are quite dramatic throughout regions in China. For example, northern Manchuria averages –13°F (–25°C) in January, compared with the average of 68°F (20°C) on Hainan Island in southern China during the same month. On the other hand, the temperature contrast between these areas is less pronounced during summer months, with an average July temperature of 70°F (21°C) in northern Manchuria and an average of 84°F (29°C) in Hainan. The lowest temperature ever recorded in China was –61.6°F (–52°C) during January at Mohe in Manchuria; the highest ever recorded in the country was 121°F (49.6°C) in July at the Turpan Depression—called the "Area of Fire" by the Chinese.

Just as temperatures in China vary greatly from region to region, so do levels of precipitation. Overall, annual precipitation averages almost 25 inches (629 millimeters), but the interior of China receives on average just 6.4 inches (162 mm); the southeast, by contrast, can expect to get about 35 inches (896 mm) of precipitation each year. The ratio between annual precipitation in the southeast through southwest and in the dry northwest is about 40 to 1.

The boundary line between China's moderate humid region and its moderate dry region runs from the Greater Xinanling Mountains through Lanzhou to Lhasa (the capital of the Tibet Autonomous Region). The boundary between the humid region and the moderate humid region runs from the Qinling Mountains to the Huai River. About 32 percent of China is in the humid region, 18 percent lies in the moderate humid region, and 31 percent lies in the dry region.

Annual wind patterns in China directly affect the amount of precipitation its regions receive. Winds coming from the north and from the high-altitude northwest interior bring cold, dry air, while winds from the south and east bring moist, warm air. During sum-

China's Geography at a Glance

Location: Eastern Asia, bordering the East China Sea, Korea Bay, Yellow Sea, and South China Sea, between North Korea and Vietnam

Area: approximately the same size as the United States
   total: 3,704,427 square miles (9,596,960 sq km)
   land: 3,599,994 square miles (9,326,410 sq km)
   water: 104,432 square miles (270,550 sq km)

Borders: Afghanistan, 47 miles (76 km); Bhutan, 292 miles (470 km); Burma, 1,358 miles (2,185 km); India, 2,100 miles (3,380 km); Kazakhstan, 953 miles (1,533 km); Kyrgyzstan, 533 miles (858 km); Laos, 263 miles (423 km); Mongolia, 2,906 miles (4,677 km); Nepal, 768 miles (1,236 km); North Korea, 880 miles (1,416 km); Pakistan, 325 miles (523 km); Russia, 2,265 miles (3,645 km); Tajikistan, 257 miles (414 km); Vietnam, 796 miles (1,281 km)

Coastline: 9,010 miles (14,500 km)

Climate: extremely diverse; tropical in south to sub-arctic in north

Terrain: mostly mountains, high plateaus, deserts in west; plains, deltas, and hills in east

Elevation extremes:

   Lowest point: Turpan Pendi—505 feet (154 meters) below sea level
   Highest point: Mount Everest—29,035 feet (8,850 meters)

Natural hazards: frequent typhoons (about five to seven per year along southern and eastern coasts); damaging floods; tsunamis; earthquakes; droughts; land subsidence

Source: Adapted from CIA World Factbook, 2004.

mer months, warm air from the south meets cold, dry air from the north to create a great deal of precipitation.

Rainfall between May and October accounts for 80 percent of China's annual precipitation. Changing prevailing winds also create great variation in precipitation levels in the same area, especially in the Lower Yellow River Basin. In south and southeast China, typhoons often sweep through the area in summer. During years in which typhoons are more frequent, annual precipitation is far higher here.

China's regions vary greatly in altitude—another factor that affects its variations in climate. Altitude varies from 505 feet

The desolate Turpan Depression, located in the Xinjiang Uygur Autonomous Region, is the lowest and hottest place in China.

Number 3 or Number 4?

Until 1996, the CIA World Factbook—a compendium of statistical information about all the world's countries—ranked China as the third largest by area, behind only Russia and Canada. While some geographical publications continue to give China's rank as third, the CIA World Factbook now places it fourth, slightly behind the United States. The change stems not from the fact that China lost territory or the United States gained new territory. Rather, in 1997, the CIA World Factbook began using another—and supposedly more authoritative—source, the Statistical Abstract of the United States, for determining U.S. total area. That source says the United States comprises 3,717,812 square miles (9,629,091 sq km); the World Factbook had previously accepted the figure of 3,618,784 square miles (9,372,610 sq km). China, by comparison, is listed at 3,704,427 square miles (9,596,960 sq km).

In any event, China and the United States are comparable in size, regardless of which is really the world's fourth-largest country and which is the world's third-largest country. The difference between the two, as currently listed in the CIA World Factbook, is about the size of Maryland and Delaware combined.

(154 meters) below sea level in the Turpan Depression in northwestern China to 29,035 feet (8,850 meters) at the peak of Mount Everest on the China-Nepal border—the highest elevation in the world. Two-thirds of China is composed of mountains and highlands, which tend to have more extreme climates than do areas of lower elevation.

Heavenly Lake (Tianchi Lake) is nestled high in the Tian Shan Mountains of western China's Xinjiang Uygur Autonomous Region.

China's Land and Topography

China is by far the largest country of eastern Asia. From east to west, it spans more than 60° of longitude, from the confluence of the Heilong River and the Wusuli River (longitude 135° E) to the Pamirs (longitude 73° E). Calculating China's latitudinal span (north to south) is not quite as straightforward. From the Heilong River (latitude 53° N) at the border with Russia, north of Mohe, to Zengmu Reef (latitude 4° N) at the southernmost tip of the Nansha Islands, China's territory spans more than 49° of latitude. But ownership of the Nansha Islands is disputed. Measured from the Heilong River north of Mohe to the southern tip of Hainan Island, China stretches through only about 35° of latitude.

The Chinese government claims that its sea territory extends 12 nautical miles out from land. That means that all the sea within 13.8 miles (22.2 km) of the Chinese coastline or of the Chinese islands falls within Chinese sovereignty. By this definition, China has a total maritime area of 1.8 million square miles (4.73 million sq km). This includes, from north to south, the Bo Sea, the Yellow Sea, the East China Sea, and the South China Sea, as well as part of the Pacific Ocean east of Taiwan.

The Bo Sea is China's only continental sea; the other three are technically parts of the Pacific Ocean. Since most of China's coastline is quite flat, it has excellent harbors. Many remain ice-free year-round.

China also claims about 6,500 islands of more than 500 square meters (5,382 sq ft) in size. According to the National Bureau of Statistics of China, the largest island in the country is Taiwan, which China claims as a territory but which currently operates autonomously; it measures more than 13,900 square miles (36,000 sq km) in total area. The second largest is Hainan Island, which measures 13,125 square miles (34,000 sq km).

The Evolution of Modern-Day China

China was one of the earliest cultural centers and among the earliest established states in the world. Its first documented cultural center evolved under the Xia dynasty (ca. 2200–ca. 1700 B.C.) in the lower Yi-Luo River valley in the western part of today's Henan Province. Archaeological evidence found in what was once the capital, Erlitou, suggests that a substantial geographical area fell under the rule of the Xia dynasty. Throughout most of its history, China has been ruled by dynasties, except in the period before the Xia era, when leaders were chosen from among elite wise men and not within family bloodlines, as with dynastic rule. The earliest dynastic culture began in the North China Plain; the practice later spread from China to Japan and Korea, then to Southeast Asia. Over the past 4,000 years, China's culture, along with the territory under the control of Chinese empires, gradually spread outward from the North China Plain. Again and again, China was divided, but it always reunited into a single entity.

China and Its Neighbors

Fourteen countries share a border with China. Five of them—Mongolia, Russia, Burma (Myanmar), Kazakhstan, and India—have borders with China that extend more than 1,000 miles (1,609 km).

The borders of China have evolved through thousands of years as the result of complicated political, military, racial, and economic changes. Over the centuries, China has been involved in numerous border disputes with its neighbors, and some remain unresolved today. In western China, a portion of the mountainous Pamirs area claimed by China has not been confirmed by border agreements with the neighboring countries of Pakistan, Afghanistan, and Russia. The border China shares with Russia (formerly the Soviet Union) has caused almost constant conflicts between the two countries. Along segments of the Ergun, Heilong, and Wusuli Rivers, both countries have stationed massive numbers of soldiers. The countries engaged in periodic border clashes throughout the late 1960s and early 1970s. In the 1980s, Soviet leader Mikhail Gorbachev adopted a moderate position toward China in a speech he delivered in 1986 at Vladivostok—a city that the Russians had taken from China toward the end of China's Qing dynasty (1644–1911). The two countries resumed border negotiations, which had been halted in protest by China when the Soviet Union invaded Afghanistan in 1979. China and the Soviet Union agreed to resolve their differences in the northeastern sector of the border first. In 1997, China and Russia (the Soviet Union had collapsed in 1991) signed a preliminary border agreement, and in October 2004 they concluded an agreement delineating the entire border.

China also disagrees with India over the border around Aksai Chin, north of Kashmir, which is controlled by China but claimed by India. Another large area in dispute lies south of what is called the McMahon Line, a border that the occupying British drew in 1914 as the Sino-Indian border along the Himalayas. The line, named after British negotiator Henry McMahon, was agreed to by Tibet and Great Britain at the end of the Simla Conference of 1913–1914. It runs from the eastern border of Bhutan along the crest of the Himalayas, to the great bend in the Yaluzangbu River.

This border was never marked clearly, however. The People's Republic of China never recognized the British-defined border, and China claimed rights to a large area that is currently under the control of India. This dispute led to a border war in 1962 between the two most populous countries in the world. According to official casualty reports, India lost more than 3,000 soldiers (dead or missing) in the monthlong war; China did not reveal its casualties, but they are believed to have been substantial as well.

After the 1962 conflict, India argued that China was controlling some 12,750 square miles (33,000 sq km) of India's territory in the Aksai Chin region. China countered that India was occupying 34,750 square miles (90,000 sq km) of its land, and it also claimed Arunachal Pradesh, India's easternmost state, as its own territory. In 1980, China proposed to settle the problem by accepting the McMahon Line in exchange for India's conceding the Aksai Chin area to China. But India refused. Since then, the two countries have had many talks on the issue, but as of late 2004, negotiators were still trying to agree on "guiding principles" to address the boundary dispute.

Meanwhile, China and Vietnam both lay claim to two small island groups in the South China Sea: the Xisha Islands (also called the Paracels) and the Nansha Islands (better known to the rest of the world as the Spratly Islands), portions of which are also claimed by Malaysia and the Philippines. Chinese troops currently occupy the Xisha, which are surrounded by potentially significant underwater

Soldiers march along the disputed border between China and India. In 1962 the two countries went to war over the region known as Aksai Chin.

oil and natural gas reserves. China is also in a dispute with Japan over ownership of Diaoyutai (Japanese: Senkaku) and Chiwei Islands in the East China Sea. In addition, a border conflict between China and Vietnam flared in the 1970s, turning these once-friendly Communist neighbors into enemies. Their relationship improved during the 1990s, and they have since signed a treaty settling the border dispute.

Other neighboring countries with which China has successfully concluded border agreements include Nepal, Mongolia, North Korea, Afghanistan, Laos, Kazakhstan, and Kyrgyzstan. A border survey is under way between China and Kazakhstan and between China and Kyrgyzstan. Burma and China signed the Boundary Treaty in 1960 and finished a mutually satisfactory border inspection in 1987.

One political and territorial issue that remains unresolved, and could potentially explode, is the status of Taiwan. Consisting of one large island and a handful of small outlying islands, Taiwan lies across the Taiwan Strait from mainland China's Fujian Province. In 1949, when the Chinese Communist Party, led by Mao Zedong, emerged victorious in a civil war for control of China, members of the defeated Kuomintang, or KMT (known in the West as the Nationalist Party), fled to Taiwan. There, under the authoritarian leadership of Chiang Kai-shek, the Nationalists reestablished the Republic of China government, which they claimed was the legitimate government of all of China. The mainland People's Republic of China, meanwhile, regarded (and still regards) Taiwan as a renegade province. As Chiang fatuously vowed to "recover the mainland," the Chinese Communists threatened to "liberate" Taiwan by force if necessary. Despite periodic escalations in the rhetoric, war never came, however. Over the decades, Taiwan developed a vibrant capitalist economy and a democratic, multiparty political system. In 1999, the KMT lost power to the pro-independence Democratic Progressive Party in free elections, and since that time the possibility of declaring independence has been raised. In the event of such a declaration, Beijing has refused to rule out the use of force to reunite Taiwan with the mainland.

From the Roof of the World to the Sea

China is a land of varied terrain, with marked topographical contrasts. It contains the world's highest mountain range as well as one of the world's lowest depressions. In general, though, China's terrain descends from west to east in what might be thought of as three large steps.

In the west lies the top step, the Qinghai-Tibet Plateau. This vast tableland covers about 850,000 square miles (2,201,500 sq km) and includes the Tibet Autonomous Region as well as parts of the Xinjiang Uygur Autonomous Region, Qinghai Province, and Sichuan Province. Average elevation is approximately 13,125 feet

(4,000 meters) above sea level. Tibet itself is the highest region in the world, averaging about 16,000 feet (4,875 meters). Its scenic valleys drop only to about 12,000 feet (3,660 meters); mountain passes exist between 14,000 and 18,000 feet (4,270 and 5,500 meters), and it is not unusual for the mountain ranges themselves

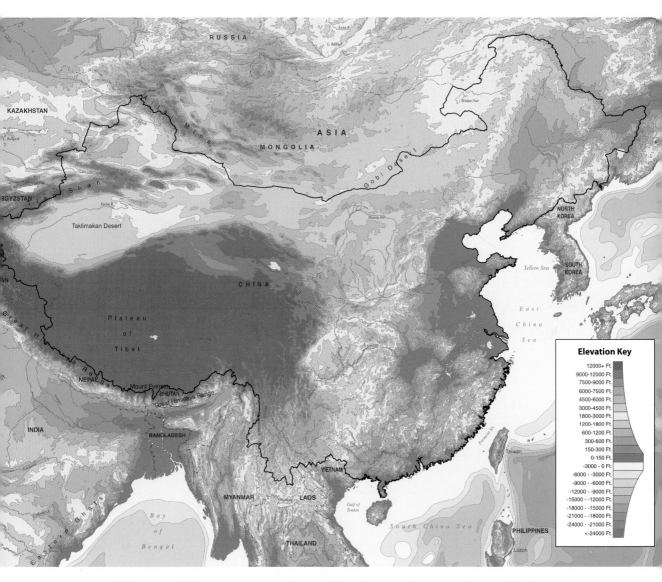

Western China is composed mostly of rugged mountains and plateaus (and, in the north, desert). Low-lying plains cover much of the country's easternmost third.

An aerial view of Mount Everest, the highest mountain in the world. Rising 29,035 feet (8,850 meters), Everest is located on the border between Nepal and China's Tibet Autonomous Region.

to soar 20,000 to 24,000 feet (6,100 to 7,300 meters). Tibet is also home to the Himalayas, the world's tallest mountains. Rising above all the other peaks is Mount Everest, earth's highest mountain. Called "Chomolangma" in the Tibetan language, Everest soars 29,035 feet (8,850 meters) above sea level at its summit. Tibet certainly deserves its nickname—the Roof of the World.

East and north of the Qinghai-Tibet Plateau, the land descends to what might be thought of as China's second major topographical step. This step includes the gently sloping Inner Mongolia Plateau, the Loess Plateau, the Yunnan-Guizhou Plateau, the Tarim Basin, the Junggar Basin, and the Sichuan Basin. Some of the land is still quite high—reaching about 12,000 feet (3,660 meters)—but elevations are more likely to be in the 2,000-to-6,500-foot range (610–1,980 meters). In addition, there are several significantly lower areas, including parts of the Sichuan Basin in Sichuan Province and the Turpan Depression in Xinjiang

Uygur, which contains China's lowest point at 505 feet (154 meters) below sea level.

China's third major topographical step extends east to the coast. Though it is interspersed with hills and foothills—and, particularly in the south, some low mountains—this band of terrain consists mainly of low-lying plains. These include, from north to south, the Northeast China Plain, the North China Plain, and the Middle-Lower Yangtze Plain.

Overall, mountains, hills, and plateaus account for 65 percent of China's total land area. China has one of the highest mean altitudes in the world; 33 percent of the country is mountainous, while only 12 percent is plains. The area of China that lies below 500 meters (1,640 feet) almost equals the area higher than 3,000 meters (9,842 feet); each constitutes about one-quarter of China's total land area.

China's varying natural environments contribute to the variety of agricultural methods used by its people. The topography of the country is such that most of the water system runs west to east and empties into the Pacific Ocean. Exceptions are those systems that originate on the southern Qinghai-Tibet Plateau; these run north to south and drain into the Indian Ocean, or they empty into the Pacific Ocean from the barrier of the Hengduanshan Mountains.

How China Uses Its Land

China has about 236.3 million acres (95.6 million hectares) of arable land. However, arable land per capita is only about one-third of the world's average, and dry regions account for more than half of China's total land area.

Most of the country's arable land is concentrated along the Northeast China Plain, the North China Plain, the Middle and Lower Yangtze River Plain, the Pearl River Delta, and the Sichuan Basin. The Northeast China Plain is famous for its fertile black soil, which nurtures crops of wheat, corn, soybeans, Chinese

Ethnic Kazakhs race horses across the grasslands near Yining, in north-western China. The traditionally nomadic people of the grasslands raise horses, cattle, and other livestock.

sorghum, sugar beets, and flax. The North China Plain is very flat, with a deep soil layer. This encourages production of wheat, corn, millet, Chinese sorghum, cotton, and fruits, including apples, pears, grapes, and persimmons. The Middle and Lower Yangtze River Plain is famous for its rice, broad bean, rapeseed, orange, tangerine, and freshwater fish production. It is sometimes referred to as "the Hometown of Fish and Rice."

Grasslands account for some 988 million acres (400 million hectares) in China. About 556 million acres (225 million hectares) of this is usable for farming and ranching. Grasslands extend from the northeast to the southwest for about 1,865 miles (3,000 km). Inner Mongolia is the biggest natural ranch in China. It is known for its Sanhe horses, Sanhe cattle, and Mongolian sheep. Another important natural livestock industry lies in the Heaven Mountains in Xinjiang. China's renowned Yili horses and Xinjiang fine-wool sheep are raised here.

Forests cover 331 million acres (134 million hectares) of China, or 13.9 percent of its land. This is a far lower percentage than the world's average of 22 percent (the figure for the United States is 33 percent). Moreover, forestland is unevenly distributed in China. The Greater and Lesser Xinan Mountains and Changbai Mountains in the northeast are the largest forested areas. The most abundant trees are red pine and larch, and broad-leaf trees such as birch, poplar, elm, and Manchurian ash. In the southwest forests of China, fir, teak, dragon spruce, and Yunnan pine are common, as are unusual species such as red sandal, camphorwood, nanmu, and padauk.

China contains almost 36 million acres (15 million hectares) of highlands, mostly in the north Qinghai-Tibet Plateau. This is sparsely used for grazing of livestock. Deserts, including the formidable Gobi Desert and the Taklimakan Desert, account for 158 million acres (64 million hectares) of China's territory, and 106 million acres (43 million hectares) are rocky mountains in the dry northwest and the Qinghai-Tibet Plateau.

Permanent glaciers occupy 11.5 million acres (4.67 million hectares) of China; these are mostly in the west and northwest, which is where most of the country's rivers and streams originate. Rivers, lakes, reservoirs, and swamps make up about 92.2 million acres (37.33 million hectares) in China.

At 243 feet (74 meters) high and 266 feet (81 meters) wide, Huangguoshu in China's central Guizhou Province is the largest waterfall in Asia. The Baishi and Dabang Rivers feed the waterfall.

China's Water and Mineral Resources

China has many rivers, streams, and lakes and is home to the world's fifth-largest freshwater resources. About 66 million acres (approximately 27 million hectares) of China are waterways or bodies of water. Rivers and streams account for 30 million acres (12 million hectares), lakes for 19.7 million acres (8 million hectares), and man-made water bodies (including reservoirs and ponds) for 16.4 million acres (6.67 million hectares). China also has abundant mineral resources—the country ranks third in the world in total mineral reserves; 149 different minerals have been confirmed to exist in China.

The Watery East

Ninety-two percent of China's water resources are located in the east. But the relatively young, high mountains in the country's western regions are the birthplaces of glaciers. About 43,000 glaciers, covering about 14.5 million acres (5.87 million hectares), provide a kind of water reserve that equals the volume of all water flow in the entire country. The glaciers in China provide resources for surface and underground water.

The annual water flow of China is more than 5 percent of the world's total. China has about 680,000 megawatts (mW) of potential hydroelectric energy—the largest potential in the world. More than half of this amount is exploitable; it could produce 1.9 trillion kilowatt (kW) hours. However, northern and western China have few water resources. China's challenge is to maintain a sustainable level of development for its hydrological resources in the future. Among those resources are its four seas, which present many opportunities for future electrical generation.

China's Rivers

The Yangtze River is called "Changjiang" or "the Long River" in Chinese. It certainly earns its name. The Yangtze is the most important waterway in China and is the third longest in the world, after the Nile River in Africa and the Amazon River in South America. Originating in the Qinghai-Tibet Plateau, the Yangtze River flows through some of the most populated parts of China along its 3,915-mile (6,300-km) run to the East China Sea. Most of the river is navigable; oceangoing ships can sail from its mouth all the way to Wuhan—a distance of about 620 miles (1,000 km). Smaller ships can navigate even farther upstream, to Chongqing in Sichuan Province.

The river nurtures 694,984 square miles (1.8 million sq km) of heartland, including the Middle and the Lower Yangtze River Basins, which are home to about 300 million people. The basins are famous for their high levels of rice and wheat production. At the mouth of the Yangtze River is China's largest city, Shanghai. The

The vast majority of China's rivers lie in the eastern half of the country.

Sichuan Basin, near the upper part of the Yangtze River, has been called "the Kingdom of Heaven" by the Chinese because its mild, humid climate and fertile soil make it a prolific crop-producing region. Sichuan Basin crops include many types of grains, soybeans, tea, and sugarcane, as well as many kinds of fruits and vegetables. Isolated from other regions by the mountains surrounding it, the basin historically was a kingdom of its own, set apart from the main Chinese empire.

The middle section of the Yangtze River stretches from the Sichuan Basin to Hubei Province, cutting through a series of mountain areas about 15 miles (24 km) long. Here, some parts of the river are less than 360 feet (110 meters) wide, creating one of the greatest wonders of China—the scenic Three Gorges. Three Gorges is one of the most frequently visited sites in China. It is also the place where a huge and controversial project, the Three Gorges Dam, is currently under way.

The government of China began building the world's largest dam at Three Gorges after its leader, Deng Xiaoping, approved the massive project in the 1990s. The dam rises about 590 feet (180 meters) above the valley floor and is about 1.3 miles (2.1 km) wide. At completion, it is supposed to provide between one-tenth and one-eighth of China's electrical power and is expected to decrease electrical shortages in the fast-developing Pearl Delta cities of southern China.

The Three Gorges Dam is also supposed to end the Yangtze River's severe flooding problems, enhance navigation, and increase

A view above the giant sluice gate of the Three Gorges Dam at Yichang shows the area that was flooded when the gate was closed in June 2003. The Three Gorges Dam is the largest water-control project in history; it took nearly 10 years to build the dam, at a cost of approximately $25 billion.

development in the heartland of China. The project has involved an enormous number of laborers and much investment. It has also required the relocation of at least 1.5 million local residents. Once the reservoir behind the dam fills completely, much of the scenery and historic sites in the Three Gorges area will be underwater and will essentially no longer exist. The impact of sedimentation from upper stream soil erosion resulting from deforestation has been a major concern for engineers of the dam. The long-term environmental impacts of the project remain to be seen.

The Yellow River, the second-longest river in China, has been called "the Cradle of Chinese Civilization." Called "Huanghe" in Chinese, the river is named for its yellowish color, which occurs as a result of loess, a yellow soil blown into the region from Inner Mongolia. Loess is light, loose, and loamy and is therefore easily carried by wind. Much of the Yellow River is not navigable because of its heavy levels of sedimentation.

The Chinese also refer to the Yellow River as "Xuan He," meaning "the river above the ground," since the sedimentation has accumulated over thousands of years and has caused some parts of the riverbed to rise several meters higher than the surrounding ground. Over time, a man-made riverbank has been built to match the rising riverbed. During the wet season, the Yellow River is prone to major flooding.

The Pearl River is an important artery in south China, measuring about 1,375 miles (2,214 km) in length. It nurtures one of the fastest-growing areas in China—the Pearl Delta, where some of China's greatest and most important cities are located. Hong Kong, Shenzhen, Macao, Guangzhou, and Zhuhai are all in the Pearl Delta region. The Grand Canal, also known as the Jinghang Canal, runs from the capital city of Beijing in the northern Pearl River area to Hangzhou on the southeast coast. Canal construction began more than 2,000 years ago and eventually helped link the north

The Yellow River, the second-longest river in China, runs through the city of Lanzhou, in Gansu Province.

and the south. Running 1,119 miles (1,801 km), the Grand Canal is the longest and the oldest man-made waterway in the world. It links five major rivers in China—the Heilong, the Yellow, the Huai, the Yangtze, and the Qiantang. Because it is narrow and shallow, however, it is not navigable for large vessels.

In total, China's many rivers flow about 267,200 miles (430,000 km). About 62,140 miles (100,000 km) of China's rivers are suitable for navigation.

China's river systems can be grouped into one of two categories: exterior or interior. Rivers with exterior systems are those that empty into larger bodies of water such as oceans or seas. The Yangtze, the Yellow, and the Pearl are exterior rivers that flow into the Pacific Ocean. The Yarlungzangbo River, which originates in Tibet, flows eastward before curving to the south and emptying into the Indian Ocean. This river also flows through one of the largest canyons in the world, the Yarlungzangbo Canyon, which is 313.5 miles (504.6 km) long and 19,714 feet (6,009 meters) deep. The Ertix River originates in Xinjiang and flows northward to empty into the Arctic Ocean—the only river in the country to flow into this ocean. Rivers with interior systems eventually empty into desert or salt marsh regions. At 1,354 miles (2,179 km), the Tarim River in the southern Xinjiang Autonomous Region is the longest interior river system in China.

China's river basins are large, but most of its rivers are concentrated in the south and southeast. Only a few rivers run through interior China; these make up less than 5 percent of China's total river volume.

Most of China's rivers also run through highlands and gorges where elevation differences are high and water flow is rapid. This means that they have a high potential for generating hydroelectric energy. In most of the lower-elevation streams of China, waterbeds are wide, so the water tends to flow more slowly. These low-elevation waterways are useful for agricultural irrigation, fisheries, and transportation.

The Many Lakes of China

China has about 24,900 lakes. Among them, 2,800 are larger than 100 hectares (247 acres) and 13 are larger than 100,000 hectares (247,105 acres). The majority of China's lakes are in the Lower Yangtze River Basin and the Qinghai-Tibet Plateau. Eastern China's freshwater lakes account for 45 percent of the country's total lake area; most of China's saltwater lakes are in the west. The biggest freshwater lakes in China are the Dongting, Boyang, Tai, Hongze, and Cao, which are also called the Five Large Lakes. Lake Qinghai in the northwestern province of the same name is the largest saltwater lake in China, measuring 1,132,484 acres (458,300 hectares).

As with China's rivers, some of its lakes are suffering from the effects of development. Dongting Lake, for example, has been over-fished, resulting in a severe decline in diversity of fish species. The total surface area of Lake Dongting shrank from 1,679 square miles (4,350 sq km) in 1949 to 1,011 square miles (2,619 sq km) in 1983 because of continuing subsidence (lowering of the earth's surface caused by factors such as compaction and decrease in groundwater levels) and extensive reclamation of farmland from the lake.

The Seas of China

Four seas are near China's mainland: the Bo, the Yellow, the East China, and the South China. The Bo Sea is the only enclosed sea in China. It covers about 31,000 square miles (80,000 sq km) but is very shallow, with an average depth of only 59 feet (18 meters). With an area of about 146,720 square miles (380,000 sq km), the Yellow Sea has an average depth of 144 feet (44 meters). It extends eastward to the Korean Peninsula, southeastward to the Sea of Japan, west and northward to mainland China, and southward to the East China Sea. At 297,300 square miles (770,000 sq km) and with an average depth of 1,145 feet (349 meters), the East China Sea is surrounded by mainland China, Taiwan, the Korean Peninsula, and the islands of Japan. The East China Sea links to the Sea of Japan in the east; in the southwest it links to the South China Sea through the Taiwan Strait.

The South China Sea is the biggest sea bordering China; it measures approximately 1.3 million square miles (3.5 million sq km), with a maximum depth of 17,641 feet (5,377 meters). The South

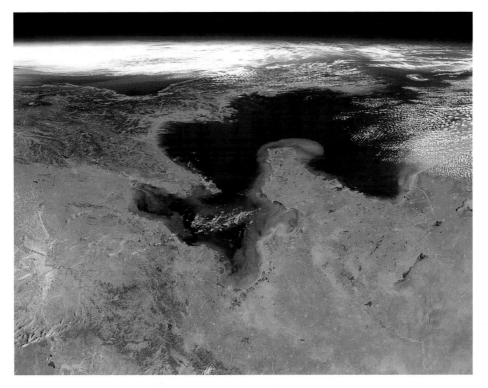

The Bo Sea is pictured at the center of this satellite image. China's Shandong Peninsula juts into the waterway from the lower right; behind it are the Yellow Sea and the Korean Peninsula.

China Sea extends northward to mainland China and Taiwan, eastward to the Pacific Ocean through the Balintang Channel and also to the Sulu Sea through the Balabac Strait, southwestward to the Indian Ocean through the Strait of Malacca, and southward to the Java Sea through the Karimata Strait. It is a heavily trafficked body of water, full of ships from around the world.

China's seas contain valuable natural resources, including salt, minerals, oil, and natural gas. China is the world's largest producer of sea salt, and 80 percent of its output is produced in the north, at Liaoning, Changlu, Shandong, and Jiangsu. North China has mainly straight coastlines with gently sloping sea floors and conditions that are favorable to salt production. China also has some smaller salt production facilities in the south.

A Land Rich in Minerals

China has an abundance of minerals; deposits of 20 of them are among the highest in the world. These include coal, iron, copper, aluminum, stibium, molybdenum, manganese, tin, lead, zinc, and mercury.

China mines about 2 billion tons of coal per year and has total recoverable deposits that may exceed 1 trillion tons. Major deposits exist in Shanxi Province, the Inner Mongolia Autonomous Region, and Xinjiang. The country also has 46.35 billion tons of iron ore, mainly in the northeast, north, and southwest. China's reserves of rare earth metals far surpass the combined total for the rest of the world. It also has abundant reserves of petroleum, natural gas, oil shale, phosphorus, and sulfur. Petroleum reserves are concentrated in the north and on the continental shelves of the East China Sea. China holds more than 200,000 discovered mineral deposits, including more than 440 oil and gas fields and 16,000 other solid mineral deposits.

China is self-sufficient in, and may be able to export, 19 minerals. They include coal, tungsten, tin, molybdenum, sodium, rare earth metals, graphite, fluorite, magnesium, barite, talcum, gypsum, diatom, cement rock, and silicon dioxide. It is nearly self-sufficient in iron ore, manganese, vanadium, zinc, bauxite, nickel, brimstone, phosphorus, uranium, and asbestos. Important mineral resources that China must import include oil, copper, gold, and silver.

Energy Resources

China's has the world's third-largest reserves of coal, after Russia and the United States. At today's mining levels, China's coal reserves could last for approximately 500 years. Of its existing deposits, 12 percent are clean, non-bituminous coal; 75 percent are bituminous coal; and the rest is brown coal. China's coal

A worker sorts processed coal at a mine outside of Taiyuan, in northern China.

China contains a wealth of natural resources. Shown here is an oil refinery in Lanzhou.

industry is healthy enough not only to meet its own needs, but also to export in great quantities.

China's oil and gas resources are quite large. Yet demand for oil to power the country's booming economy far exceeds domestic production; indeed, China's oil imports doubled between 1999 and 2004. As of 2002, China's proven oil reserves totaled 26.75 billion barrels. Most of this petroleum is in the west, around the Tarim, Qaidam, and Zhunger Basins. Other significant oil fields are located in the South China Sea, near the mouth of the Pearl River; in the Yingehai Basin, southeast of Hainan Island; and in the Bo Sea.

The East China Sea is also believed to contain significant amounts of petroleum. China's proven reserves of natural gas, as of 2002, were estimated at 1.29 trillion cubic meters. One-quarter of this total is found in the Tarim Basin, which also holds one-seventh of China's proven oil reserves.

In addition to its oil, natural gas, and coal, China also has plentiful uranium reserves. This radioactive element is used in the production of nuclear energy (as well as nuclear weapons). Thus far, China's discovered uranium reserves are clustered around the border of Jiangxi, Hunan, and Guangxi, near the Nanling Mountains.

The giant panda's distinctive black and white coloring makes it one of the world's most easily recognizable species. The giant panda is native to southwestern China, living in the provinces of Sichuan, Gansu, and Shaanxi along the eastern edge of the Tibetan plateau. However, destruction of the bamboo forests where the giant pandas live has brought the species to the brink of extinction.

4

The Plants and Animals of China

China is one of the most biologically diverse countries in the world. According to the Biodiversity Committee of the Chinese Academy of Sciences, China is home to more than 5,000 species of vertebrates—about one-tenth of the total number of vertebrate species in the world. More than 32,000 species of higher plants are found in China as well. Nearly every major plant of the frigid, temperate, and tropical zones of the Northern Hemisphere grows in China. Seven thousand species of woody plants, including 2,800 species of trees, also thrive in China.

China's Native Trees and Plants

China's ecosystems are numerous and varied. They include coniferous forests, broadleaf forests, shrub and shrub-meadow regions, steppes, savannas, deserts, tundra, alpine regions, meadows, marshes, and aquatic

Towering pines cover the lower slopes of the Tian Shan Mountains.

vegetation regions. Within these ecosystems are areas that differ from one another based on soil types, latitude, humidity levels, and other natural features. For example, depending on latitude, the East Monsoon Zone of China holds tropical rainforests, monsoon forests, subtropical evergreen broadleaf forests, warm-temperate deciduous broadleaf forests, temperate broadleaf and coniferous mixed forests, and sub-temperate coniferous forests. The same variation is found among longitudinal regions of China; for example, northern China has forests, steppes, and deserts, varying from east to west. A region with one of the most widely varying ecosystems is China's Qinghai-Tibet Plateau. Ecosystems in this area range from mountain forests to alpine deserts.

Some plant types exist only in China. They include the metasequoia, the Chinese cypress, the Cathaya (an evergreen), the China fir, the golden larch, the Fujian cypress, and the dove-tree. The metasequoia, an extremely tall redwood, is the only living species in the genus *Metasequoia*. It is often called a "living fossil" because it was first discovered as a fossil from the Mesozoic era. In 1948, however, scientists learned that a small stand of an unidentified tree discovered in China was actually a new living species of the fossil. Harvard University eventually sent an expedition to China to collect seeds from the newly discovered species, and the seedlings that grew from this collection were distributed to universities and arboretums around the world for study and experimentation. In the United States, the metasequoia is often called the dawn redwood or China redwood. While the bark and foliage of the metasequoia are similar to those of other redwoods, it is a deciduous tree, not an evergreen.

Another so-called living fossil is the ginkgo, also known as the maidenhair tree. Once thought to be extinct, the ginkgo was rediscovered in China in the mid-1700s. Since then it has been planted throughout the world. Fossils of this ancient species, believed to be more than 150 million years old, have been found in the United States, Europe, and Greenland. Many scientists believe that the ginkgo we know today is a cultivated version, and that the original species no longer exists in the wild. Others believe that wild ginkgoes might still exist in the mountains of eastern China.

In Chinese, the ginkgo is called "YinXing," which means "silver-colored apricot tree." This description comes from the appearance of its white seed, encased in an oval-shaped, slimy tan-orange fruit. Ancient Chinese records also described the ginkgo as "Ya-zhi-tou" (a tree with leaves like a duck's foot). The ginkgo is dioecious, which means that its trees are either male or female. Only the female tree, when fertilized, produces the rather smelly fruit. The Chinese systematically planted ginkgo trees for many years; some living ginkgo trees in China are more than 500 years old, and several have been preserved in temple gardens. Today, extracts of ginkgo are believed to provide relief for several ailments, including circulatory problems, short-term memory loss, headaches, ringing in the ears, and depression.

In addition to its many varieties of trees, China also has more than 5,000 species of plants. About 2,000 of these are edible, and many have medicinal properties. Chinese herbal treatments that have been used since ancient times include ginseng from the Changbai Mountains, notoginseng from Yunnan and Guizhou, Chinese wolfberry from Ningxia, and safflower from Tibet.

Flowering plants are also bountiful in China. One of the most elegant native flowers is the peony, whose blooms are cherished as having the "color of the nation and the scent of heaven." Also called "the king of flowers," the peony is characterized by large, many-petaled blossoms in rich colors. Two other native flower species, the Yunnan azalea and the Tibetan primrose, are widespread in southern China. During their flowering season, tourists flock to mountain slopes carpeted in their blossoms.

China's Animals

China is home to about 1,185 species of birds, 500 species of mammals, 375 reptile species, and 280 amphibian species, according to the Chinese Academy of Sciences. In addition, there are approximately 2,800 fish species in Chinese waters. Among the more than 100 species that are unique to China are the giant panda, the South China tiger, the brown-eared pheasant, the red-crowned crane, the golden-haired monkey, the white-flag dolphin, and the Yangtze alligator.

The giant panda lives in temperate-zone mountainous bamboo forests in central China, around the Yangtze River area. One of the most easily recognized but rarest animals in the world, the giant panda has become the symbol for endangered species and conservation efforts worldwide. Today, only about 1,000 giant pandas live in the wild in China; another 120 are in captivity in Chinese breeding facilities and zoos. About 20 other giant pandas are in zoos in other parts of the world.

The Chinese call the giant panda "Da XiongMao," meaning "large bear-like cat," or "Da MaoXiong," meaning "large cat-like bear." The gentle animal has a special place in Chinese culture: it has been considered a symbol of peace for thousands of years. It is said that warriors 2,000 years ago would raise a flag emblazoned with the image of the panda to request a temporary halt to fighting. The practice seems to have survived through the centuries: in February 1972, after the historic Shanghai Communiqué was agreed upon by the People's Republic of China and the United States, China offered a pair of giant pandas to the National Zoo of the Smithsonian Institution in Washington, D.C., as a gesture of peace.

With a docile disposition and a heavy, cuddly-looking body similar in size to that of an American black bear, the giant panda is so beloved that some U.S. zoos rely on their star panda exhibits to bring in revenue that is also used to help save other endangered animals. Giant pandas stand between two and three feet tall at the shoulder when on all four legs, and they can be up to six feet long. Males in the wild weigh up to 250 pounds (113 kilograms); females rarely reach 220 pounds (100 kg).

A far different kind of endangered species is China's red-crowned crane, a graceful, mostly white migratory bird that stands about five feet (1.5 meters) tall. Its name comes from the distinctive patch of red on the top of its head.

The white-flag dolphin, also found only in China, is one of just two species of freshwater whales in existence. A male white-flag dolphin was caught in the Yangtze River recently, the first time one had been captured. Local legends, however, include tales of

A visitor to the Zhalong Crane Nature Reserve runs up behind a red-crowned crane in order to encourage it to fly, as one of the reserve's animal keepers looks on. The establishment of the nature reserve has helped to increase the population of the rare red-crowned crane.

white-flag dolphins that chased fishermen's boats and caused them to overturn.

China's Livestock

According to the National Bureau of Statistics of China, the country's livestock population reached 670 million in 1999. The country's agricultural region is mainly in six provinces, which account for the great majority of China's livestock.

The most important of these animals is the pig, which plays a vital role in the country's farming industry. By one estimate, China has 51 percent of the world's pig population, and the number of pigs in the country has increased dramatically over the last half century, from 88 million in the early 1950s to 430 million today. Most of China's 60 breeds of pigs are stall-fed. The Tibetan pig is an exception: this breed usually grazes on grassland, in flocks of 60 to 80.

The ancient Chinese were fond of the wild boar (an ancestor of the domesticated pig), admiring its speed and strength. As the wild boar became domesticated, rural inhabitants learned that it was easy to feed, did not require a great deal of space, and provided not only food, but also fertilizer and other useful products. "The treasure is all around the pig," one traditional saying goes. Before the beginning of the Qin dynasty in the third century B.C., eating pigs was a mark of high status—only kings and nobles dined on the animal's flesh. Pigs were also symbolically important in Chinese rituals; at funerals, for example, the effigy of a pig and the bones of an actual animal were often included in the burial site of a deceased loved one to provide good company. Today, pigs are still celebrated in Chinese statues and images that symbolize prosperity, although the number of pigs held on family-run farms has decreased as commercial processing increases.

Another important type of livestock in China is cattle. The 55 breeds of cattle in China fall into one of three ecological-geographic groups. Northern cattle, such as the Mongolian breed, are well adapted to grazing in the steppe and meadow regions. Cattle of the central plains have adapted to the flat agricultural land of the deciduous broadleaf forest region and are mostly stall-fed, with some grazing. Cattle in China's southern region, by contrast, have adapted to the region's hilly tropical and subtropical climates. These include Hainan, Guangxi, and Yunnan breeds.

Pigs and cattle may be the most important and abundant livestock in China, but the country is also home to several other types, including horses, camels, sheep, and goats. Used as draft animals in China since ancient times, horses are still used for plowing fields and for recreational riding. Seventy breeds of horses live in four ecological-geographic groups in China: the North Grasslands, the Xinjiang Mountain Grasslands, the Qinghai-Tibet Plateau, and the Southwest Mountains.

Bactrian camels are tied up outside the Sunday market in Kashgar, Xinjiang. Camels are still used for transportation in China's desert regions.

Many people are surprised to learn that camels are used for transportation in China's desert regions. Most of China's camels are of the double-humped Bactrian variety, although a few single-humped camels live in southern Xinjiang. Camels feed mostly on natural grassland, with some exceptions in the winter. In addition to providing transportation, they are also used for wool.

China's 35 breeds of goats are easily adaptable to a variety of environments; thus, they can be found nearly everywhere. In an attempt to recover some of the country's overgrazed grassland areas, the Chinese government is recommending that all goats be stall-fed rather than left to graze. Still, the sheep of China are the major grazers. Four types—the Mongolian, the Kazakh, the Tibetan, and the Central Plain lineages—live mostly in China's temperate areas.

Garbage rots along the banks of the Yellow River in Yan'an, Shannxi Province. Pollution is a major problem in China, as rapid economic growth has led to severe degradation of the environment.

Environmental Concerns

Like many other countries that have undergone rapid industrialization and economic development, China suffers from major environmental problems, including massive pollution and the deterioration of ecosystems. In addition, China faces frequent natural disasters, which are costly in terms of loss of human life and property and which often adversely affect the health of China's ecosystems.

Pollution in China

While pollution is a problem throughout China, it is most severe in cities. According to the World Bank, China is home to 16 of the world's 20 most polluted cities. Air pollution is of particular concern. Of 300 cities tested by China's State Environmental Protection Agency in 2002, nearly two-thirds failed air-quality standards set by the World Health Organization. For many Chinese, the consequences are severe: lung disease is China's leading cause of death; an estimated 300,000 Chinese die prematurely each year of respiratory disease.

China's main sources of air pollution are industrial and residential combustion of coal, which releases dust, carbon dioxide, and sulfur dioxide (of which China has the world's highest emissions). Among the most dangerous air pollutants are total suspended particles (TSPs)—molecular toxin clusters less than 100 microns (one-tenth of a millimeter) in diameter. They include lead, aerosols, smoke, fumes, dust, fly ash, and pollen. TSPs are so small that they can penetrate deeply into human lungs, where they are highly likely to cause illness. Concentrations of TSPs and sulfur dioxide are higher in the northern regions of China, during the winter, and in residential and industrial-commercial areas. Densities peak during morning and evening rush hours.

A large volume of pollutants in the atmosphere can result in a haze or smog, and can increase the likelihood of more people developing cancer and respiratory problems such as asthma and bronchitis. It has also been suggested that high levels of TSPs and sulfur dioxide (or a mixture associated with these pollutants) may have contributed to a higher than average number of premature births among pregnant women in Beijing.

China's high levels of sulfur dioxide emissions contribute to another problem: acid rain. About 25 percent of the country suffers acid rain, which damages plant and aquatic life. And the problem appears to be increasing: the number of cities experiencing acid rain more than 40 percent of the time it rained was up by more than 7 percent between 2002 and 2003, and the number of metropolitan areas that had no acid rain at all decreased.

China still has considerable problems with clean drinking water: 26 out of 47 cities monitored did not meet the national standard for

Heavy pollution hangs in the air over Beijing. China's growing prosperity has allowed greater numbers of people to own automobiles, and this has contributed to an increase in air pollution throughout the country.

good water quality. Water pollutants in China include acid, alkaline, salt, and organic waste. The worst water pollutants of all are the types of organic wastes that do not dissolve easily. In the 1990s, total annual emissions from industrial and urban waste in cities topped 35 billion tons. Industrial waste accounted for more than 70 percent of the country's water pollution problems.

A layer of slime and rubbish floats on the surface of Hong Kong's Victoria Harbour.

China suffers from a shortage of waste-treatment plants, although the government has recently promoted significant expansion in this area. Still, the official target for wastewater treatment in 2005 was set at only 45 percent of the total wastewater generated in urban areas.

A report published in China in the 1980s stated that more than 82 percent of its rivers and lakes were polluted. The water quality of larger rivers such as the Yangtze, the Yellow, and the Pearl is slightly better than that of smaller waterways such as the Hai, the Liao, and the Songhua, where quality indices have all been worse than the national standard level. Sixty-nine percent of the urban regions of 94 rivers evaluated in the 1990s were polluted.

Large freshwater lakes and reservoirs tend to have higher water quality than do rivers and streams. However, these bodies of water have another problem: they are suffering from the effects of a process called eutrophication. This is a condition in an aquatic ecosystem where high nutrient concentrations stimulate blooms of algae. Although eutrophication is a natural process in the aging of lakes and some estuaries, the effects of human activities—agricultural runoff, urban runoff, leaking septic systems, sewage discharges, eroded stream banks, and similar sources—can greatly accelerate the process. The nutrients overstimulate the growth of algae, clouding the water and blocking sunlight. The underwater grasses that die off as a result become unavailable to aquatic creatures that rely on them for food and shelter. When the algae die and decompose, they use up oxygen, which is essential to most organisms in the water.

Eutrophication is especially severe in East Lake in Wuhan, Lake Cao in Anhui, and Lake Dianchi in Yunnan. China has worked hard in the last 10 years to reduce heavy-metal waste from industry, which contributes to this process. The major pollution today comes from industrial organic waste and untreated urban waste. Agricultural runoff from chemical fertilizers such as nitrogen and phosphorus has increased the eutrophication problem in lakes and bodies of water near cities.

Chinese industrial solid waste is another problem. National statistics in 1995 reported that the country had accumulated 5.9 billion tons of industrial solid waste occupying 135,900 acres (55,000 hectares) of land. Recycled industrial solid waste accounted for only 31 percent of this total amount; the rest was dumped in landfills or in rivers, lakes, and seas. Of China's urban waste, only 2.3 percent was treated; the rest was disposed of in landfills or buried lightly. Untreated urban waste has become a major environmental problem and is affecting China's urban development.

Ecosystem Deterioration

Whole ecosystems are deteriorating in China. Along with air and water pollution, China has to contend with increasing deforestation, degeneration of grassland, soil desertification and erosion, and soil loss. The cycle of deterioration began with a period of uncontrolled deforestation over the past several decades. Although the Chinese government began an advocacy program for planting new trees after the 1960s, many more trees were cut down than were planted over the ensuing decades. Deforestation is worsened by factors such as forest fires, diseases, and insect pests, and by conversion to farmland to meet the country's growing demand for food. The result is habitat loss, near extinction, and in some cases total extinction of some of China's unique plants and animals. The result of deforestation is quite stunning: less than 14 percent of China's total land area is now forested.

China also faces severe degeneration of its grasslands. Of the country's more than 1 billion acres (417 million hectares) of grassland, 543.6 million acres (220 million hectares) are already given over to agriculture and other uses. Each year, 3.3 million acres (1.33 million hectares) of grassland are lost to overgrazing, outdated land management practices, disease, and rat overpopulation.

Soil desertification is especially problematic in northern China. The 11 provinces in this region have 39 million acres (15.8 million hectares) of land at risk of severe soil desertification. China's Bashang region, north of Zhangjiakou, is the most threatened of all. Population and industry growth, urban sprawl, overplanting, overgrazing, and overlogging are contributors to vegetation loss and deforestation here, as elsewhere. To date, 907 million acres

A Chinese worker tends to shrubs being planted on the edges of the Gobi Desert, in an attempt to stop soil from being blown away. Desertification has become a major problem in China, particularly in naturally dry northern areas.

(367 million hectares) of land have been affected by soil erosion—more than 38 percent of China's total land.

Soil loss along China's rivers reaches 5 billion tons per year. Forty million tons of nitrogen, phosphorous, and potassium are also lost from China's soil annually. Since the People's Republic of China was established in 1949, the country has lost 6.6 million acres (2.67 million hectares) of arable land. Severe soil erosion has caused decreased agricultural productivity; 89 percent of the inhabitants of China whose incomes fall below the country's poverty level live in regions of extreme soil loss and erosion.

China's Plans for Improving the Environment

Under the Chinese constitution, the country is obligated to "protect and improve [the] living environment and ecosystem" and to "protect precious fauna and flora, as well as [to apply] reasonable application of natural resources." Since 1980, the Environmental Protection Law of China has been incorporated into its five-year national plans. These plans list targets and procedures for treating industrial waste, improving water quality, improving environmental quality, and restoring ecosystems. The country's goal is to balance economic development with environmental protection—but at present, China's annual investment in solving the problems of the environment is comparatively low.

Among the methods China uses to try to minimize human impact on the environment is to control population growth. The government has enforced a one-child policy for families, with some exceptions in rural areas and among minority groups, since the 1970s. It has also encouraged couples to marry later and have children later.

A cyclist rides past a billboard in Beijing that reads, "Control population growth, and raise the quality of the population." Since the 1970s, the government of China has attempted to limit the growth of the country's population through such measures as a one-child-per-couple policy, in part to lessen the strain on the environment.

The policy helped to slow the country's population growth rate, but its frequently harsh enforcement methods drew criticism and caused great controversy throughout the world. China views population growth not only as a social issue but also as an economic one, but many believe that to solve the problems of the environment and the economy, limiting families to one child is not enough and does not address the heart of these issues.

Model Counties, Shelterbelts, and Water Conservation

The Chinese government has taken other steps to improve the environment. It has made some strides in industry pollution prevention and treatment by establishing more waste treatment plants and by increasing industrial waste treatment rates and emission standard approval rates.

China has begun a program of nominating model "Xian" (counties) for ecosystem protection. By 1995, ecosystem protection in these counties reached 17.3 million acres (7 million hectares).

In the past few decades, China has also been working on a program of establishing shelterbelts—barriers of trees and shrubs that protect against wind and reduce soil erosion. Although the program has been slowed somewhat by investment problems, parts of some already established shelterbelts have begun to show results. The Sanbei shelterbelt project is among them. This shelterbelt begins in Binxian in Heilongjiang Province and extends westward to the Wuzibieli Mountains in Xinjiang, passing through 551 counties in 13 provinces and autonomous regions. When complete, the total Sanbei shelterbelt will cover about 86.5 million acres (35 million hectares), including the heavily eroded areas of the Inner Mongolian desert and the Loess Plateau. Another shelterbelt project covers the Upper and Middle Yangtze River Basin. This project will pass through 645 counties in 13 provinces or regions, including

Yunnan and Sichuan. The total area of the completed shelterbelt will be more than 395 million acres (about 160 million hectares). The objective of these shelterbelt programs is to plant more forest, protect existing forest, increase forest cover throughout the country, and decrease soil loss and soil erosion. Between 1989 and 2000, the project planted about 30 million acres (12.1 million hectares) of trees. About 100 counties in China have already seen positive results.

China's water conservancy projects have also helped increase irrigation and control flood waters. The government has erected 83,000 reservoirs and 6.2 million dams, with a total water volume of 1.5 trillion cubic feet (450 billion cubic meters). Reservoirs, dams, water gates, and flood-division regions have all helped to form a coordinated system of flood control in China—but the program is far from perfect. Some of the reservoirs themselves have had a negative environmental impact because of sedimentation and water quality problems. This is due in part to poor construction practices, particularly with older structures in the water conservation system.

Overall, however, China's established conservation projects have helped control pollution, erosion, and flood problems. Whether this continues depends on how well the country is able to maintain and improve on these ongoing projects. Ecosystem management is a complex and costly venture. How much China's individual projects will help with the country's severe environmental problems remains to be seen.

Protecting Animal and Plant Life

The Chinese government has established 932 national nature reserves, with a total area of more than 195.2 million acres (79 million hectares), in an effort to protect forests and wildlife. The reserves place many rare and endangered species of wildlife under legal protection. Twelve of these reserves—including the famous

Wolong in Sichuan, which was established to protect giant pandas—belong to the "International People and Biosphere Protection Network," a group of national organizations devoted to protecting natural resources. Qinghai's Bird Island and Lake Dongting, along with four other reserves, have been listed as among the world's most important wetlands. It is estimated that China's nature reserves have benefited 70 percent of the country's ecosystems, 80 percent of its animal species, and 60 percent of its higher plant species.

In 1994, China proposed an "Action Plan for the Conservation of Biodiversity," which provided guidance for various ecological and environmental protection activities. The country has established genetic resource preservation facilities to collect (and thus preserve) genetic materials from thousands of species, and results are promising. Species extinction has slowed somewhat, and some plant and animal species appear to be recovering. For instance, before China established four nature reserves to protect the Cathay silver fir, only 3,000 were known to exist. Today, Hunan Province alone boasts 30,000 Cathay silver firs.

Similar advancements have been made in saving endangered animals from the brink of extinction. So far, the country has established 250 wild animal breeding centers specializing in rescuing seven major species, including the giant panda and the crested ibis. As of 2004, the Center for the Protection of Giant Pandas, located in the Wolong Nature Reserve, had successfully bred 37 giant pandas. The number of crested ibises in China has increased from 7 to 248. Likewise, the number of artificially bred Yangtze alligators in China is nearing 10,000, and the Hainan slope deer population has grown to more than 700 from just 26 in the early 1980s. Relict gull populations have increased five-fold, to more than 10,000, in less than 15 years.

Chinese law mandates punishment for all activities aimed at destroying wild animal resources, and in extremely serious cases the death penalty is an option. Still, China is battling enormous odds. Lack of enforcement of conservation laws, coupled with three decades of explosive economic growth, have put much of China's wildlife and ecosystems in jeopardy.

Natural Disasters

China suffers nearly every imaginable type of natural disaster, including earthquakes, floods, landslides, avalanches, volcanic eruptions, wildfires, insect infestations, famines, hurricanes, droughts, and desertification. Since 1949, the country has experienced an annual average of 7.5 droughts, 5.8 floods, 7 typhoon landings, 1.3 earthquakes of magnitude 7.0 or higher, and 100 landslides; it has also experienced severe crop disease once every three to four years. Plant diseases and insect infestation have affected an average of 19.7 million acres (8 million hectares) each year, and grassland insect pests damage an average of 49.4 million acres (20 million hectares) annually.

In the 20th century, 6.1 million people in China died as the result of earthquakes—more than in any other country in the world. Between 1949 and 1992, earthquakes injured 8.3 million Chinese people and killed 2.77 million. Between 1989 and 1992, the death toll from floods averaged 3,000 to 4,000 people annually. Landslides, debris flows, and natural collapses in China cause an average of more than 900 deaths annually.

Typhoons in China have caused massive destruction as well— more than 450 deaths between 1989 and 1992 and a direct loss of 8 billion China renmimbi, or CNY (U.S. $966.5 million in 2004 rates). Storm tides are another hazard. These extremely high tides caused by storms can cause severe damage to coastlines and to people living there. Water levels of storm tides often exceed 16.4 feet (5 meters) above normal tide ranges. Damage from 1992 storm tides in China, for example, killed 200 people and caused 9.6 billion CNY (U.S. $1.16 billion) in damages.

A Chinese rescue team searches through the rubble of a building destroyed by a landslide caused by flooding along the Yangtze River, Hubei Province. China is prone to a variety of natural disasters.

Reducing the Effects of Natural Disasters

The Chinese government is also taking steps to mitigate the effects of natural disasters. Major efforts include projects to control flooding; minimize damage from earthquakes, landslides, debris flows, and natural collapses; reduce the number of forest fires; reduce the erosion and soil loss caused by dust storms; and aid in

(continued on p. 75)

Dust Storms in Asia

At the beginning of 2001, an unusually large dust cloud drifted across the United States. It lingered over Denver, Colorado, and even obscured views of the Rocky Mountains. The dust cloud was said to have originated in northwest China—thousands of miles away.

Such dust storms are now occurring in China nearly five times as frequently as they did a half-century ago. Many scientists believe that this is proof that northwest China's once-fruitful agricultural land is eroding into desert at an alarming rate. About 900 square miles (2,300 sq km) of agricultural land in northern China—an area more than twice the size of Hong Kong—blows out of the country annually in dust clouds. As the plumes travel through Beijing and other major cities, they pick up industrial waste particles, until they become so thick that they obscure the sun, reduce visibility, and slow traffic. Roofs, field grasses, and tree leaves become coated in yellow and white dust, and people are forced to wear scarves over their faces when they venture outside. Homeowners seal windows with old rags to block the dust from seeping in. Public structures must be cleaned repeatedly during northwest China's dust storms.

Although not all of China's dust clouds have traveled as far as the United States, many of China's neighbors, including North Korea, South Korea, and Japan, have complained about the problem. The result has been the establishment of a tri-national committee to work on strategies that will alleviate the clouds. South Korea, Japan, and China have set up a monitoring and early warning system to inform one another of possible dust and sand storms moving across the continent. The United Nations Environment Programme (UNEP) is assisting them as part of a million-dollar project funded by the Global Environment Facility and the Asian Development Bank.

Solutions remain elusive. Because the storms are the result of a combination of broad factors that are difficult to control—

such as natural disasters and human interference with China's ecosystems—solving the problem of China's huge dust storms and the desertification of its farmland will be extremely difficult.

The spread of the Gobi Desert has contributed to dust storms that have increasingly become a problem for China and its neighbors. This satellite image shows a dust storm over eastern China, Korea, the Yellow Sea, and the Sea of Japan.

This satellite image shows a typhoon off the coast of China. In a typical year, five to seven typhoons can be expected to make landfall in China.

eradicating diseases that affect the country's agriculture and animal husbandry.

In China, programs to mitigate the effects of earthquakes, for example, include strengthening and reinforcing buildings and infrastructure such as railroad systems, bridges, power plants, communication lines, pipelines, and oil refineries. Preventing and treating disease that strikes crops and affects farm animals is a major undertaking. China has 28,000 biological disease treatment teams and 2,400 forest plant disease prevention and immunization agencies, employing 11,000 experts.

Despite all the precautions and enhanced disaster prevention programs, natural disasters still cause enormous annual economic losses in China—about 3 to 6 percent of the country's gross domestic product (GDP)—not to mention the loss of life, which can be in the thousands annually.

A picture of China's most famous modern leader, Mao Zedong, watches over visitors to Beijing's Tiananmen Square. In addition to serving as China's capital, Beijing is the country's educational and cultural center.

China's Cities, Regions, and Tourist Sites

China is divided politically into eight official regions: the Northeast, North China, Middle China, South China, East China, the Northwest, the Southeast, and the Special Administrative Regions (Hong Kong and Macao). Within these divisions are 23 provinces (including Taiwan), five autonomous regions, two special administrative regions, and four centrally administered municipalities (Beijing, Tianjin, Shanghai, and Chongqing). In terms of economy and tourism, however, China can also be divided into three distinct areas: the coastal region, the interior, and the deep interior.

This map of China shows the boundaries of provinces and autonomous regions, as well as major cities and important regional centers.

The Booming Coast

China's coastal region is the main source of its economic boom. The provinces and municipalities of Liaoning, Hebei, Beijing, Tianjin, Shandong, Jiangsu, Shanghai, Zhejiang, Fujian, Guangdong, Guangxi, and Hainan all run along China's coasts. From Liaoning to Guangdong Province and Hainan Island, one sees construction cranes nearly everywhere. The area is under intense urban and industrial development. The region's infrastructure is being updated to attract more businesses and tourists. In the cities, some old and historically significant buildings have been demolished to make way for high-rise towers; in rural regions, many farmers have abandoned land that has been in their families for generations to live and work in one of the newer factory towns or cities. Most of the funding for this development comes from overseas investment and from China's central government.

Parts of China's coastline are being developed into resort areas. Among the most popular are the beaches of Beidaihe, Qingdao, and Tianya and Haijiao. Two of China's islands attract many visitors as well: the exotic Snake Island west of Dalian, known for its snake populations, and nearby Bird Island, which attracts birdwatchers.

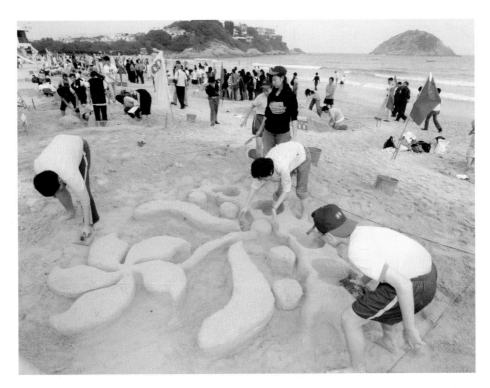

Chinese students take part in a sand sculpture competition on a beach in Hong Kong. In recent years, other parts of China's coast have been developed into beach resorts.

Beyond China's Coasts

China's non-coastal areas include the majority of its provinces and autonomous regions. Not as heavily developed as its coast, these regions in general are dominated by agricultural and industrial economies rather than tourism. The Sichuan Basin, the Middle and the Lower Yangtze River, the Northeast Plain, and the North China Plain are among the most fertile agricultural lands in the country.

China's deep interior region includes the Xinjiang Uygur Autonomous Region and the Tibet Autonomous Region. Xinjiang, which makes up one-sixth of China's total land area, is the country's largest provincial-level political entity. It is also one of the most sparsely populated regions in China, with a density of only about 4.4 people per square mile (11.5 people per sq km).

Xinjiang is located along the ancient route from China to western Asia, the Middle East, and Europe—the famous Silk Road, one of the world's most historically important trade routes. The area's geography consists of two basins and three mountain ranges—the Dzungaria Basin, sandwiched between the Altai and the Tian Shan (or Heaven) Mountains, and the Tarim Basin, which lies between the Tian Shan and the Kunlun Mountains. The Tarim Basin is the largest inland basin in the world. Taklimakan Desert is the largest desert in China. Qogir Peak, which soars to 28,250 feet (8,610 meters) at the border of China and Pakistan, is part of the Kunlun Mountains, the western part of which is referred to as the Karakoram Range. Qogir Peak, nicknamed "K2," is the second-highest peak in the world after Mount Everest. Xinjiang has 10,000 glaciers—more than any country in the world except Poland.

Xinjiang is one of driest places in the world, with an average annual precipitation of less than 6 inches (145 millimeters). Eighty percent of agriculture in Xinjiang depends on irrigation from the region's 320 rivers. Xinjiang also has 139 lakes, including Bosten

China's Xinjiang Uygur Autonomous Region encompasses a large area of sparsely populated land in western China. The Silk Road, an ancient network of trade routes that connected China and the civilizations of the Mediterranean Sea, passed through the region. This ornate building is the Aba Khojak Mosque in Kashgar.

Lake, the country's biggest inland freshwater lake, famous for a fishery that produces about 1,000 tons of fish annually. The region's beautiful scenery has spurred increasing numbers of tourists to visit the area, and the Bosten Lake area hosts a newly built amusement park.

At about 500 feet (152 meters) below sea level, the saltwater Aidin Lake is the lowest lake in China and the second-lowest body of water in the world, behind the Dead Sea. The beautiful Tianchi Lake in the Tian Shan Mountains is sometimes called Heavenly Lake because of its high elevation—the lake sits more than 6,230 feet (1,900 meters) above sea level and is surrounded by historic sites; it is also a popular destination for visitors who love ice sports. Swan Lake in Xinjiang, higher than the Heavenly Lake at about 8,200 feet (2,500 meters), was named after the many thousands of swans that spend the summer there. The swans are protected in a national nature reserve.

Xinjiang is rich in oil, coal, and other mineral resources. Its residents practice irrigation and oasis agriculture. The region is China's largest producer of long-staple cotton. It also produces some of China's finest fruit, including grapes, watermelons, peaches, cherries, and the famous Hami melon. Xinjiang is a hub for animal husbandry centers as well.

Tibet, "the Roof of the World," has often been regarded by outsiders as a mysterious land, largely because of its isolation and the religious beliefs of its inhabitants. Traditional Tibetan society was dominated by Lamaism, a form of Buddhism that emphasized the importance of monastic life and that had a hierarchical structure of authority. At the top of that hierarchy was the Dalai Lama.

China's role in Tibet has created much controversy internationally. Although the Chinese assert that Tibet has been part of their country since the Yuan dynasty (1278–1368), Tibet exercised de facto autonomy in the first half of the 20th century. After the founding of the People's Republic of China, the threat of military force brought Tibet under Chinese control, and several Tibetan uprisings were suppressed with considerable loss of life. Today, many Tibetans and international human rights activists charge that the

Chinese government is attempting to destroy traditional Tibetan culture by promoting Chinese migration to the region.

Most of the 2.4 million Tibetans are farmers. Tourism is a growing industry in Tibet, with hotels and shops springing up in larger cities such as the capital, Lhasa. A railway between Lhasa and Sichuan is under construction.

Beijing

China's capital city, Beijing, is not only the country's political center but also part of a new economic development zone, along with

The Temple of Heaven, built in 1420 during the Ming dynasty, is a famous tourist attraction in Beijing. China's emperors offered sacrifices to heaven once a year, to give thanks for the past year's blessings and ask for favorable conditions in the next year.

Tianjin and Tangshan. Geographically, Beijing's size depends on the definition of its city limits. The city's center, which is enclosed by the Beijing City Wall, covers 24 square miles (62 sq km); the size of Beijing's political administrative region, which includes eight other counties, is 6,486 square miles (16,800 sq km). The population of the area within the political boundary of Beijing totaled 14.5 million by the end of 2003.

Beijing was established in 1045 B.C. during the Eastern Zhou dynasty; the Jin dynasty later made it the country's capital. The city is home to 5 of China's 27 World Cultural and Natural Heritage

This photo shows a small part of the Imperial Palace in Beijing, constructed during the rule of the Qing dynasty emperor Qianlong (1736–1796). Only two of the massive complex's buildings remain today; hundreds of other buildings were destroyed during wars in the 19th century. In the fall of 2004, the Chinese government announced plans to reconstruct the complex.

sites, including the Forbidden City, the Great Wall, the Peking Man Ruins, the Summer Palace, and the Temple of Heaven. The city also contains more than 200 other sites of historical and cultural interest, including Tiananmen Square, Taihe Palace (the emperor's official administrative building), and Lingen Palace in Changling (a mausoleum for an emperor of the Ming dynasty).

Beijing has long played a unique role as the center of Chinese politics, culture, and education. Today it is home to 67 universities, more than 500 research institutes, and 26 national labs.

Shanghai

Shanghai, which claimed 16.74 million residents in 2001, is the largest city in China and the most popular among foreign visitors. Centrally located along China's north-south coastline near the mouth of the Yangtze River, Shanghai is the showcase of the country's phenomenal economic growth. It offers a bonanza of tourist attractions, business opportunities, and cultural activities.

The city's deepwater port makes it an excellent hub for convenient transportation—but Shanghai has undergone many transformations. Early in its history, Shanghai was a fishing village. In A.D. 1292, the Yuan dynasty established Shanghai as a county. Three centuries later, during the Ming dynasty, Shanghai transformed itself into a textile manufacturing center. After the Qing dynasty established a customs house there in 1685, Shanghai became a popular trade center. It is now known as an industrial and financial center that retains colonial influences from previous incarnations.

Official city government statistics show that Shanghai's area has increased tenfold since the early 1950s, to 2,448 square miles (6,340 sq km). It now has 18 divisions and one county within its administrative area, and it also administers three islands at the mouth of the Yangtze River, including Chongming Island, the third largest in China. The delta city is flat and low in elevation, rising an

Shanghai is China's largest city, with a population of more than 16 million. It is also the center of China's booming economy.

average of only 13 feet (4 meters) above sea level. Eleven percent of Shanghai's total area is water. The main body of water within the city boundary is the Huangpu River, along with its tributaries, the Suzhou and Chuanyang Rivers. Originating from Lake Tai, the Huangpu is about 70 miles (113 km) long. About 1,180 feet (360 meters) wide on average and ice-free year-round, the Huangpu is an excellent transportation resource for Shanghai.

The surrounding area's soil is fertile, with some 822,000 acres (333,000 hectares) of arable land in Shanghai's suburban counties. Crops include rice, wheat, cotton, oil-bearing seeds, and vegetables. Shanghai ranks among the highest in the country in yield per unit of staple crops. Animal husbandry in the suburbs has developed rapidly, and native products such as mushrooms, garlic, rabbit hair, frozen fowl, flash-frozen vegetables, whitebait, and crab-fry are popular export products.

Shanghai's large and highly skilled workforce, broadly based scientific establishment, tradition of industrial cooperation, and excellent transportation and communications facilities have all contributed to the city's stature as the leading industrial center in China. It produces a variety of capital and consumer goods, including specialized dies, lathes, electronic assembly equipment, watches, cameras, radios, fountain pens, glassware, leather goods, stationery products, and hardware. The city's well-established chemical and petrochemical industries serve as a basis for the production of plastics, synthetic fibers, and other products. Textile manufacturing is also significant.

Shenzhen

The city of Shenzhen is situated in the southern coastal area of Guangdong Province, about 100 miles (160 km) from Guangzhou and about 22 miles (35 km) from Hong Kong, near the influx of the Pearl River to the west. This strategic location was a large part of the reason Shenzhen was selected as a special economic zone

(SEZ)—an area where foreign investment and capitalism were encouraged under the reforms of Chinese leader Deng Xiaoping. The city faces the sea and is surrounded by mountains, but its western region is mainly hills and plains.

The story of Shenzhen has no counterpart in the modern world. A fishing village with a population of about 20,000 in the 1970s, it has some 3 million residents today. Visitors to Shenzhen are reminded of Hong Kong's skyline of high-rise buildings, although Shenzhen seems to have been built almost overnight. Its phenomenal growth can be attributed to the Chinese government's policy of giving favorable economic incentives to its designated special economic zones, and to foreign investment from Hong Kong, Japan, and Taiwan, as well as its access to cheap labor from all over the country.

Hong Kong: A Powerhouse of the Pacific

Hong Kong is an Asian wonder. Located south of mainland China, the city is actually made up of 235 islands, including Hong Kong, Jiulong, and Xinjie. It borders Shenzhen in mainland China along the Shenzhen River. With a total area of 12,000 square miles (1,096 sq km) and 6.5 million people, it is one of the most densely populated cities in the world, averaging 15,330 people per square mile (5,930 people per sq km).

Historically, Hong Kong was under the administration of Guangdong Province's Xinan County until 1840. At the close of the First Opium War—a one-sided conflict between China and Great Britain in 1839–1842—the British government signed a treaty with the Qing dynasty and gained control of Hong Kong Island and South Jiulong. In 1898, Britain signed another treaty to lease Xinjie and nearby islands from China for 99 years. During World War II, the Japanese occupied Hong Kong, but the British regained control after the war ended in 1945. In 1984, the British and Chinese governments signed a bilateral agreement leading to a peaceful transfer

A railcar carries tourists to the top of Victoria Peak, Hong Kong.

of control from Great Britain to China on July 1, 1997. Currently a special administrative region of China, Hong Kong continues to operate as a "free economy" under China's "one country, two systems" policy.

Hong Kong's stature as a center for international trade, shipping, finance, tourism, and communication makes it vital to the interests of China as a whole. It is the largest container port in the world and the headquarters of the world's largest independent commercial fleet. For 10 years, Hong Kong's airport has been the second-largest processor of trade goods. The city's new international airport, completed in 1998, has perhaps the world's largest enclosed space in one of the most energy-efficient buildings ever created.

In 1995, Hong Kong became a member of the World Trade Organization, with trading privileges with 220 countries. About 972 foreign companies have Asian-Pacific headquarters in Hong Kong, making the city a true financial bridge between mainland China and the rest of the world. At the same time, mainland China has become Hong Kong's largest trade partner. Hong Kong is also the world's third-largest financial center, behind New York and London. It has a complex but well-established financial market, including a market for foreign currency, loans, stock exchanges, insurance, and gold.

It is no surprise that Hong Kong's strong international ties are part of the reason for its unique cultural mix. Duty-free shopping, high-quality services, and close accessibility to mainland China make it one of the most popular destinations for tourists and business travelers to Asia. Tourism is its second-largest industry, taking in the equivalent of U.S. $11.5 billion in 1996—the highest amount in Asia and the eighth largest in the world. It is an international communications center, and though its status as a manufacturing hub has declined, it is still a major producer of exports, including electronics, clocks and watches, clothing, and plastic toys.

Hong Kong is facing problems with future development. Its short-age of water is a major drawback to growth. Area rainfall varies sea-sonally, and surface water per capita is only about 8 percent that of neighboring Guangdong Province. During the explosive growth of the 1950s, water shortages became so severe that residents had 24-hour access to clean water only 40 to 50 days a year. In 1964, the Chinese government approved the construction of the Hongsheng Water Supply Project to provide water from the Dongjiang River to Hong Kong; the project has since been expanded three times. Water from the Dongjiang accounts for more than 70 percent of the fresh water supply in Hong Kong today; however, the same river also supplies water to Guangzhou, Shenzhen, Huizhou, and other cities in southern China. With economic development booming in these areas, cities are competing with Hong Kong for limited water resources.

With a shortage of usable land, reclamation has been one of Hong Kong's major strategies for continuing development. Historically, that strategy has been successful in promoting eco-nomic growth in Hong Kong. Its 15,320 acres (6,200 hectares) of reclaimed land account for about 5.7 percent of Hong Kong's total land area. The majority of reclaimed land has been given over to port, airport, and road facilities. But the environmental impact of the reclaimed land is hard to ignore. Port Victoria is the project's biggest victim—its total area has shrunk from 17,300 acres (7,000 hectares) to 10,380 acres (4,200 hectares), a loss of 40 percent. The now-crowded port experiences higher waves, worse sailing condi-tions, and a heavier population, which has in turn caused higher levels of water pollution than ever before.

Macao: European Influence

Like Hong Kong, Macao (also spelled Macau) is a special adminis-trative region of China, but the two differ greatly from one another.

Pedestrians walk through a busy intersection in downtown Hong Kong. Today, Hong Kong is an important center for international trade as well as a popular tourist destination.

Macao is on the southeast coast of China, west of Lingdingyang at the Pearl River Delta. It includes the Macao Peninsula and the two islands of Taipa and Coloane, which are linked by a six-lane highway. With a local population of 444,000 in 2003, Macao is crowded; in fact, its northern peninsula is regarded as one of the most densely populated areas in the world.

Macao is an open city with great diversity. More than 96 percent of its population speaks Cantonese, Mandarin, or Fujianese dialect; 2 percent of residents speak Portuguese. Macao's population is highly mobile—25 million people annually flow into and out of the region. Its population is growing at about 4 percent annually. Macao also boasts the continent's second-longest average lifespan for both men and women, at more than 78 years. Only Japan's citizens enjoy a longer average lifespan in Asia.

Macao, once named Haojin, was included within Chinese territory from the time of the Qin dynasty (221–207 B.C.). Portuguese immigrants in the 16th century established the area as an important port. In 1887, the weakened Qing dynasty signed a treaty allowing Macao to officially become a Portuguese colony, but about 100 years later, the Chinese and Portuguese governments agreed to return sovereignty to China in 1999. Since then, Macao has been categorized as a special administrative region. Like Hong Kong, Macao enjoys the fruits of the "one country, two systems" policy.

Macao today relies less on its former status as a port city than on gambling, tourism, manufacturing, real estate, banking, and insurance. The government legalized gambling in Macao in 1961, and this promoted tourism, hotel construction, and expanded transportation routes. In 1996, Macao attracted 8.15 million tourists. The tax on gambling normally generates 55 to 60 percent of all government revenue in Macao.

Macao's real estate industry accounts for about 10 percent of its economy. Labor costs are 30 to 40 percent lower than in Hong Kong, and land prices are about 60 to 70 percent lower. Its taxes are lower than Hong Kong's as well. Macao's unique Mediterranean flavor makes it extremely attractive to tourists traveling from Hispanic cultures. Moreover, it has a special relationship with the European Union, enjoying a privileged policy through Portugal. To promote future development, Macao built its own international airport through land reclamation. The new world-class airport opened in 1995, freeing Macao from reliance on Hong Kong's airport.

Macao has also been considering the construction of a deepwater port to replace the existing inner port, which has degraded from sedimentation from the Xi and Lingdingyang Rivers. The proposal under consideration suggests building a new, smaller deepwater port east of Coloane Island, where ships weighing between 5,000 and 10,000 tons can dock. It might also lease Huangmao Island near Zhuhai for a new port.

Tourists in China

Mainland China ranked fifth in the world in terms of inbound international tourists from 1998 to 2000, according to the World Tourism Organization. In 2003, a total of 91.66 million tourists traveled to China.

It is no secret that China has much for the average tourist to see. The country boasts many natural wonders. It offers archaeological sites of great importance. Many tourists are also drawn to China's long and rich culture; its arts and crafts; its food, music, and folk art; and its lovely architecture.

Natural Wonders

China's stunning natural scenery includes West Lake in Hangzhou, renowned for its beauty and known in Chinese legend as a heavenly jewel that fell to earth. The Su and Bai Causeways in the West Lake region were named after revered Chinese poets.

Among the best-known mountains of China are the "Column in the South" in Yaxian in Hainan Province and the Five Great Mountains ("Wu Yue"), which were once worshiped by emperors and pilgrims. They include "West Yue" or Mount Huashan, "Middle Yue" or Mount Songshan, "North Yue" or Mount Heng, "South Yue" or Mount Heng (spelled using a different Chinese character), and "East Yue" or Mount Taishan. Mount Taishan is a World Cultural and Natural Heritage site.

The Yellow Mountain (Mount Huangshan) in Anhui Province is another natural wonder and World Cultural and Natural Heritage site. A poet of the Ming dynasty, Xu Xiake, praised the Yellow Mountain in a poem: "No need to see more mountains after seeing the Five Great Mountains," he wrote, "however; no need to see the Five Great Mountains after seeing the Yellow Mountain." The breathtaking jagged peaks, twisted pine trees, hot springs, and "sea of clouds" make up what are known as the "Four Wonders of Huangshan." Rising 5,785 feet (1,763 meters) and covering 96.5 square miles (250 sq km), the Yellow Mountain dominates the terrain of southern Anhui Province and is home to an exceptionally broad range of animal and plant life.

Karst, Mountains, and Red Rock Formations

Karst is an area of irregular limestone in which erosion has produced fissures, sinkholes, underground streams, and caverns. China is famous for this type of formation, with about 321 million acres (130 million hectares) of karst—14 percent of China's total land area—mostly in Yunnan Province, Guizhou Province, and the Guangxi Zhuang Autonomous Region. In these areas, visitors find column-shaped rock hills, underground streams, caves, and natural bridges, often in unusual shapes. Among the most famous karst areas of China are the Guilin Hills, the Yangshuo Hills at the Li River in Guangxi, the Lunan Rock Forest in Yunnan Province, and

(continued on p. 98)

UNESCO World Cultural and Natural Heritage Sites in China

- The Great Wall (Beijing Municipality)
- The Forbidden City (Beijing Municipality)
- "Peking Man" Ruins at Zhoukoudian (Beijing Municipality)
- Mogao Caves at Dunhuang (Gansu Province)
- Qin Shi Huang Mausoleum and the Qin Terracotta Warriors and Horses (Shanxi Province)
- Mount Taishan (Shandong Province)
- Mount Huangshan (Anhui Province)
- Jiuzhaigou (Sichuan Province)
- Huanglongsi Scenic Spot (Sichuan Province)
- Wulingyuan Scenic Spot (Hunan Province)
- Chengde Mountain Summer Resort and Eight Outer Temples (Hebei Province)
- Potala Palace (Tibet Autonomous Region)
- Confucius Temple, Confucius Family Mansion and Confucius Woods at Qufu (Shandong Province)
- Ancient Buildings on Mount Wudang (Hubei Province)
- Mount Lushan (Jiangxi Province)
- Mount Emei and the Leshan Giant Buddha (Sichuan Province)
- Ancient City of Pingyao (Shanxi Province)
- Suzhou Classical Gardens (Jiangsu Province)
- Ancient City of Lijiang (Yunnan Province)
- The Summer Palace (Beijing Municipality)
- The Temple of Heaven (Beijing Municipality)
- Mount Wuyi (Fujian Province, 1999)
- Dazu Grottoes (Chongqing Municipality)
- Ming and Qing Imperial Mausoleums (Hubei and Hebei Provinces)

- Longmen Grottoes (Henan Province)
- Mount Qingcheng and Dujiang Dam (Sichuan Province)
- Xidi and Hongcun—Ancient Villages in South Anhui (Anhui Province)

This stone warrior guards the road leading to the Ming Tombs near Beijing.

Oddly shaped karst formations rise over rice paddies in Yangshuo, located in the Guangxi Zhuang Autonomous Region.

the Seven Star Rock in Zhaoqin, Guangdong Province.

China's volcanoes, mountains, and red rock formations are also popular tourist attractions. Most of the country's volcanoes are in the northeastern region; these include the Changbai Mountains. Lake Jingbo in the Changbai Mountains is renowned for its tranquil atmosphere and beautiful scenery. Mount Lushan seems to float on a sea of clouds; many Chinese movies have been filmed there. This mountain is different from most other high mountains in China because its peak is accessible by car. The resorts of Mount Lushan attract thousands of visitors annually. Chinese Nationalist

Party leader Chiang Kai-shek and Communist Party leader Chairman Mao Zedong had private resorts on this mountain. Tourists seeking to experience China's mountainous regions also flock to its red rock formations, mostly found in the south. Danxia Mountain in Guangdong, Mount Qiyun in Anhui, and Mount Wuyi in Fujian (a World Cultural and Natural Heritage site), are among the most visited red rock formations.

The Waters of China

Water and water movement hold important symbolic significance in Chinese culture. The Chinese term for paintings of natural scenery translates to "paintings of mountains and water." Among China's most scenic and well-known bodies of water are the "Five Large Lakes," Dianchi Lake, West Lake in Hangzhou, and East Lake in Wuhan. Famous man-made lakes include the Lake of

The sun sets over the Yangtze River near the Three Gorges Dam in central Hubei Province.

Thousand Islands in Zhejiang Province.

China's rivers and waterfalls include the beautiful Three Gorges at the Yangtze River, the wave wonders in the Qianchang River in Zhejiang Province, and Huangguoshu Falls in Guizhou Province— the biggest waterfall in China. Other falls include Changbai Falls in Jilin Province and Layer Falls at the Lunan Rock Forest in Yunnan Province. Among China's hot springs areas are the Laoshan Springs in Shandong and the Huaqingchi in Shanxi Province.

China's Cultural Heritage

China's millennia-old civilization makes the country rich in historical and cultural treasures. Its famous archaeological finds include the ruins at Zhoukoudian, where the "Peking Man," then believed to represent a new genus and species of human ancestor, was discovered in the 1920s. The site became a World Cultural Heritage site in 1987. Sites of similar significance include the "Nantian Man" and "Yuanmo Man" ruins. In the Banpo Village ruins, secrets of the ancient Yangshao civilization were unearthed.

The ruins of Chang'an, which may have been the largest planned city in the ancient world, surpassing even Rome, are located near present-day Xi'an. Chang'an was the capital city for the Han and the Tang dynasties. One account states that by A.D. 742, the population of Chang'an had reached almost 2 million, and the city was greater in area than present-day Xi'an. A census in 754 showed that 5,000 foreigners lived in the city, including missionaries, merchants, pilgrims, and tradespeople from Turkey, Iran, India, Japan, Korea, and Malay. Japanese students who came to Chang'an brought Chinese culture and writing to Japan and influenced that country's writing. Rare plants, spices, medicines, and other exotic goods from Western countries were traded in the city's bazaars.

Visitors to China can discover a wealth of architectural history in its many palaces, temples, mausoleums, gardens, residential buildings, mosques, pagodas, bridges, ornamental columns, memorial archways, and mansions. Perhaps the most famous palace is the Forbidden City in Beijing. This World Cultural Heritage site adheres to a strictly symmetrical design. Nine gates run along a north-south axis; the emperor's official seat is located where the north-south and the east-west axes meet. This location symbolized the unlimited power of the Chinese emperor.

China's imperial and private gardens, admired the world over, focus on carefully creating beauty without showing human influence. Imperial gardens are known for being extravagant and spacious, while private gardens are tranquil but sophisticated and follow small but exquisite plans. Examples of the former are the Summer Palace, and the Chengde Mountain Summer Resort, which are World Cultural Heritage sites.

Glossary

acid rain—rainfall that has increased acidity, generally as a result of air pollution.

arable—suitable for cultivation.

coniferous—belonging to an order of mostly evergreen trees and shrubs, many of which produce cones.

county (Xian)—a rural administrative unit in China, below the level of a province.

deciduous—belonging to a group of trees whose leaves are shed seasonally.

desertification—degradation of land in arid and semiarid areas, typically through human mismanagement or natural disaster.

eutrophication—the process by which a body of water becomes enriched with dissolved nutrients such as phosphates, typically leading to growth of algae and a reduction in the water's oxygen content, which in turn adversely affects fish populations.

gross domestic product (GDP)—the total value of goods and services produced by a country in a one-year period.

loess—a yellowish loamy soil that is easily blown by the wind.

"one country, two systems"—a policy originating in the early 1980s that was designed to promote the reunification of Hong Kong, Macao, and Taiwan with mainland China and that offered these areas a higher degree of autonomy within China as special administrative regions.

rare earth metals—any of a series of metallic elements whose oxides occur in widely distributed but relatively scarce minerals.

sovereignty—autonomy; political power over a region.

subsidence—the sinking or settling of land.

typhoon—a tropical cyclone occurring in the region of the Philippines or the China Sea.

vertebrate—any animal that has a spinal column.

Further Reading

Benewick, Robert, and Stephanie Donald. *The State of China Atlas: Mapping the World's Fastest Growing Economy.* London: Myriad, 1999.

Brown, Liam D'arcy. *Green Dragon, Sombre Warrior.* London: John Murray Publishers Ltd., 2004.

Chang, Luke T. *China's Boundary Treaties and Frontier Disputes.* London: Oceana, 1982.

China Handbook Editorial Committee. *China Handbook Series: Geography.* Beijing: Foreign Languages Press, 1983.

Leeming, Frank. *The Changing Geography of China.* Cambridge, Mass.: Blackwell, 1993.

Pannell, Clifton W., and Laurence J. C. Ma. *China: The Geography of Development and Modernization.* Washington: Winston and Sons, 1983.

Shunwu, Zhou. *China Provincial Geography.* Beijing: Foreign Languages Press, 1992.

Smith, Christopher J. *China: People and Places in the Land of One Billion.* Boulder, Colo.: Westview Press, 1991.

Winchester, Simon. *The River at the Center of the World: A Journey up the Yangtze, and Back in Chinese Time.* New York: Picador, 2004.

Yang, Zunyi. *The Geology of China.* New York: Oxford University Press, 1986.

Zhao, Songqiao. *Geography of China: Environment, Resources, Population, and Development*. New York: John Wiley & Sons, 1994.

———. *Physical Geography of China*. Beijing: Science Press, and New York: John Wiley & Sons, 1986.

Internet Resources

http://www.cia.gov/cia/publications/factbook/geos/ch.html

The CIA World Factbook's China pages provide background and statistical information on China's geography, government, economy, people, and other topics of interest.

http://www.china.org.cn/e-changshi/

An official Chinese website providing quick facts about the country.

http://www.ifce.org/endanger.html

This website, from the International Fund for China's Environment, provides information on some of China's endangered animals, along with efforts to save them from extinction.

http://www.lonelyplanet.com/destinations/north_east_asia/china/

The Lonely Planet guide to China offers basic information and photos.

Index

Numbers in **bold italics** refer to captions.

Picture Credits

Contributors

JIA LU is currently a tenure-track faculty member of the Department of Geography at the University of Wisconsin at Stevens Point. A trained city planner and architect, Ms. Lu's interests include a variety of topics related to geography, architecture, and planning. Her specialties include city and regional planning, architectural history, geographic information systems, quantitative analysis, housing, and urban economics. She currently teaches World Regional Geography, Introduction to Geographic Information Systems, and Community Planning Practices.

Ms. Lu holds a bachelor's degree in architecture and a master's degree in Community Planning from the University of Cincinnati. She is currently completing her doctoral dissertation in City and Regional Planning at Ohio State University. She has more than 10 years of working experience in government planning and architectural design agencies, including work with the Ohio Department of Development, the Transportation Department of the City of Columbus, and the Warren County Planning Commission. Her designs have contributed to the construction of a variety of buildings now standing in China, her home country.

Ms. Lu has presented and published many professional papers and is a frequent speaker at the annual symposium of the Ohio Chinese American Professional Association. She wrote a chapter for the book *Cellular Automata Model and Its Application in Planning*, scheduled for publication in 2004.

In her spare time, Ms. Lu enjoys watercolor painting. Her work was published in the 1994 edition of *Selection of Fine Art Works in Architecture*.

JIANWEI WANG, a native of Shanghai, received his B.A. and M.A. in international politics from Fudan University in Shanghai and his Ph.D. in political science from the University of Michigan. He is now the Eugene Katz Letter and Science Distinguished Professor and chair of the Department of Political Science at the University of Wisconsin–Stevens Point. He is also a guest professor at Fudan University in Shanghai and Zhongshan University in Guangzhou.

Professor Wang's teaching and research interests focus on Chinese foreign policy, Sino-American relations, Sino-Japanese relations, East Asia security affairs, UN peacekeeping operations, and American foreign policy. He has published extensively in these areas. His most recent publications include *Power of the Moment: America and the World After 9/11* (Xinhua Press, 2002), which he coauthored, and *Limited Adversaries: Post-Cold War Sino-American Mutual Images* (Oxford University Press, 2000).

Wang is the recipient of numerous awards and fellowships, including grants from the MacArthur Foundation, Social Science Research Council, and Ford Foundation. He has also been a frequent commentator on U.S.-China relations, the Taiwan issue, and Chinese politics for major news outlets.